THE
DESERTER'S
TALE

THE DESERTER'S TALE

The Story of an Ordinary Soldier
Who Walked Away from the War in Iraq

Joshua Key

as told to Lawrence Hill

Atlantic Monthly Press
New York

Published simultaneously in Canada
Printed in the United States of America

The photos on pages 232 and 233 are courtesy of Joshua Key

FIRST EDITION

Library of Congress Cataloging-in-Publication Data
Key, Joshua
     The deserter's tale: the story of an ordinary soldier who walked away
   from the war in Iraq / Joshua Key; as told to Lawrence Hill.
       p. cm.
     ISBN-10: 0-87113-954-5
     ISBN-13: 978-0-87113-954-2
     1. Key, Joshua.   2. Iraq War, 2003—Personal narratives, American.
   3. Iraq War, 2003—Desertions—United States.   4. Military
   deserters—United States—Biography.   5. Americans—Canada.
   I. Hill, Lawrence.   II. Title.
   DS79.76.K494 2007
   956.7044'38—dc22
     [B]   2006047964

Atlantic Monthly Press
an imprint of Grove/Atlantic, Inc.
841 Broadway
New York, NY 10003

Distributed by Publishers Group West

www.groveatlantic.com

07 08 09 10 11 12   10 9 8 7 6 5 4 3 2 1

I dedicate this book to my wife, Brandi Key,
and to our children, Zackary, Adam, Philip, and Anna.
I wouldn't have made it this far without them.
—Joshua Key

Contents

MAP KEY

⊙ Cities and duration of stay during Joshua Key's service in Iraq.
ALL DATES ARE IN 2003.

● Other major cities

TURKEY

Diyarbakir

Mosul

SYRIA

IRAQ

Kirkuk

IRAN

Al-Qa'im
OCT. TO MID-NOV.

Al-Habbaniyah
AUG. TO MID-SEPT.

"Green zone"
at Al-Asad
SECOND HALF OF SEPT.

Ramadi
APRIL 28 TO LATE MAY;
MID-JUNE TO LATE JULY

Fallujah
EARLY TO MID-JUNE

Baghdad

Arak

Tigris R.

Najaf

Euphrates R.

Nasiriyah

Ahvaz

Basrah

MILES

0   100   200

KUWAIT

Kuwait

PERSIAN GULF

SAUDI ARABIA

TURKEY

ISRAEL

SYR

JORDA

IRAN

AFGHAN.

EGYPT

AREA OF
DETAIL

SAUDI
ARABIA

QATAR

U.A.E.

DUBAI

OMAN

SUDAN

Red Sea

YEMEN

Arabian
Sea

Riyadh

MATTHEW ERICSON

THE
DESERTER'S
TALE

Prologue

I NEVER THOUGHT I WOULD LOSE MY COUNTRY, AND I never dreamed it would lose me. I was raised as a patriotic American, taught to respect my government and to believe in my president. Just a decade ago, I was playing high school football, living in a trailer with my mom and stepdad, working at Kentucky Fried Chicken, and hoping to raise a family one day in the only town I knew: Guthrie, Oklahoma, population ten thousand. Back then, I would have laughed out loud if somebody had predicted I would become a wanted criminal, live as a fugitive in my own country, and turn my wife and children into refugees as I fled with them across the border.

Before I could survive and escape the war in Iraq, I had to survive my own childhood. I shot a .357 Magnum on my ninth birthday, brought down my first deer by the age of twelve, and could clean, load, and shoot any of dozens of firearms that my stepfather kept in our trailer. I was an excellent shot before I was old enough to shave. I drank alcohol of every kind, trashed two cars on country roads, and fought anybody who was willing.

Even in my earliest years, I knew right from wrong. It wasn't right to kill puppies with a hammer, which is why I shot and buried a litter of pups before my grandfather could get at them in his old-fashioned way. Iraq took all of the fun out of guns for me, but even in the days when I still loved shooting I stopped hunting after dropping that deer with a four-inch bullet through the neck.

Even though I was taught that it was shameful to get licked in a fight and come home beaten, I knew it wasn't right to gang up on someone, pick on a smaller person, or keep on punching after your opponent had fallen. I knew it was wrong to attack any person who was weak or defenseless, and everything about my early years at home reinforced that belief.

We didn't have books or newspapers at home. I had heard of the Vietnam War but didn't know when or why Americans had fought in it. But I can guarantee you this: if any man had told me he had deserted our army in wartime, I would have called him a coward right to his face. There were just some things you didn't do. By the time I was in high school I felt that it would be an honor to serve my country at war, and even to die for it. I couldn't imagine any circumstances in which an American soldier would walk away from his own armed forces and so betray his country.

Looking back, I would say that many parts of my life in Oklahoma prepared me for the war in Iraq. Our two-bedroom trailer baked in the Oklahoma sun and froze in the winter, so I was as ready for extreme weather as any American. Growing up on my grandfather's forty-acre farm, I learned to fix just about anything that was broken and make pretty well anything run. I was a private first class when I went to war, but I had farm-boy skills and my officers came to count on them. I was the one they came to, over and over again, to connect air conditioners to generators, hot-wire trucks, run our own wires to Iraqi electricity lines, and assemble plastic explosives.

As a child, I watched many times as J. W. Barker— my third and final stepfather—drank himself into a stupor and beat up my mother. I grew up learning to expect abuse. J.W. loved to bring over his drinking buddies and have them watch while I worked with his guns. I used to bet them on whether I could hit a small target with a .22 rifle. While they tipped back beer I would hang a string from a tree, pull it taut by tying it to an old fire extinguisher on the ground, stand back fifty paces, and blast through the target nearly every time. At $10 a pop it was the fastest pocket money I ever earned. And I earned a good bit of it. Growing up, I shot beer bottles, Coke cans, hanging string, and snakes, and I was a fine marksman before joining the army.

But the preparation for Iraq was more than physical. Growing up poor in Oklahoma also prepared me mentally for the war to come.

I lived with my mother, brother, and father, and then a variety of stepdads, on the farm of my grandfather Elmer Porter. I often ate at his table when there was no food at home, or when my mother was too depressed to get out of bed. Elmer had fought in the Korean War and then worked for years at Tinker Air Force Base in Oklahoma City. Five other living relatives had served in the U.S. military or gone to war. I didn't think much about war, but I had no objection to it.

One time a teacher in Guthrie got a worried look in her eye, put her hand on my arm, and asked, "Is everything all right at home?" "Yes ma'am," I told her, "it's just fine, thank you." And I thought it was true. I knew plenty of people who lived harder lives than I did. One friend had parents who both ran away from home, leaving him behind to fend for himself.

School was not exactly my strong point. Nobody in my immediate family had gone beyond high school, and I didn't see the point of further studies. I had one cousin who went to college for four years and the only job he could get in Oklahoma City was managing a waffle house. Seemed like a waste of time and money to me. I didn't read in school and hated to write, but I did enjoy math.

I didn't yet know what lay in my future, but one set of strangers already did. Before I had even graduated from high school, a string of U.S. Army recruiters started showing up at our trailer, banging on the flimsy door that blew open on windy nights, and promising health insurance and higher education in exchange for military service. They were smart men, those recruiters. They didn't waste time at the doors of doctors and lawyers but came straight for me. The recruiters said I could even join the army at the age of seventeen, with my mother's signature. She chased them off the property, but the damage was done. The recruiters had planted the seed. They didn't get me for another few years, but they had made me aware that if I ever got tired of minimum wage there was always the adventure of life in the army.

Back when I was in high school, I didn't think about joining the army, and I didn't plan on going to war. Guthrie was all that I knew and all I imagined, and the things I wanted then are the things I want now: a few acres of land for the kids to play on, with maybe a horse or two, a few pigs, and a mess of chickens in a coop. Since I was a boy I have known that I wanted to make my living as a welder. There's something about welding that I loved from the first time J.W. showed me how to turn on a torch. Under your flame the metal flows like lava. You follow its movement and work with its nature. Sometimes you mess up, but that's okay. When things go wrong, all you have to do is melt down the metal and start all over again. Nobody minds. Nobody's hurt. You fix your mistakes and get it right the next time, working the lava so that things stay together. The freedom to say *No, that's not good enough, let me try again* is what I love about welding.

To this day there is no work I'd rather do than hold a welding torch. If I had my druthers, I'd move away with Brandi and our four children and get myself enrolled in the welding program in the College of the North Atlantic in Newfoundland. I've been hearing about the school for years. They say it's one of the best on the continent. But I wouldn't be ready for welding quite yet.

I still get blackouts. I still wake up screaming in the middle of the night. I take pills to keep the nightmares at bay. The dreams are like sleeping dogs, and sometimes they haunt me during the day. Recently, I was driving on a rural road and saw a cardboard box on the shoulder. Only I didn't think *cardboard box.* I thought it was a bomb, planted just for me, set there like all the explosives I set off in Iraq or that had been placed for me and my fellow soldiers. I swerved wildly onto the grass by the side of the road to get out of its kill zone, to escape the shrapnel. When I came to I was sweating and shaking behind the steering wheel.

I have never hit my wife or my children or anyone else in my blackouts, but I have been known to throw things and to rip light fixtures from ceilings. I have been known to shout words of mayhem and war, but I never remember these things when I finally come to in Brandi's arms.

The doctors call it post-traumatic stress disorder. They say I'll have it for life, and that I just have to learn to deal with it. I can only imagine what would have happened if I had not deserted the American army in Iraq. I guess it's not that hard to tell. There are only a few options. If I had gone back to war I could have been taken out by a bullet, or mortars, or a rocket-propelled grenade. I could have been forced to kill an innocent person, or more than one.

I can say with relief and gratitude that I have never killed anybody, Iraqi or American. I have enough troubles as it is living with my own demons, and I'm not sure how I would have kept on going with innocent blood on my hands. But I know there is a chance that if I had killed someone else, I would have gone on later to kill myself.

If I had returned after a two-week leave with my family, I would have had to go on raiding, arresting, and intimidating people who were like me in the most surprising ways: poor, with almost no way to escape their miserable situations. They were hungry, but they were amazingly resourceful, too. I'll never forget the image of an Iraqi man driving up to a traffic checkpoint where I stood with my weapon at the ready. The gas line in his car had been ruptured. Outside his window he was holding up a gallon of gas so that it could flow down through a rubber hose to the engine as he inched forward in the car. He was an ordinary man, using all of his ingenuity to survive in extraordinary circumstances.

I was stationed in Fort Carson, Colorado, when President George W. Bush declared war on Iraq, and within two weeks I was flying into a war zone. I wasn't happy about it, but I went willingly. I believed what my president and my commanders told me. Somebody had to rid the world of weapons of mass destruction. Somebody had to depose the evil tyrant Saddam Hussein. Somebody had to make the world safe from terrorists who had overtaken Iraq and were threatening our lives. I felt it was better for me to help do the job now rather than leave it to my own children. Even Brandi, who was left alone at home with Zackary, Adam, and Philip, said to me, "You get 'em, Josh, before they get you. Even if it's a kid. They're terrorists too." I believed her. I felt the same way. In all the military training I had received in Missouri and Colorado, Iraqis were never called people, or citizens, or men, women, and children. They were called *sand niggers, ragheads, habibs, hajjis,* and, most of all, *terrorists.* In the army of the United States of America, those were our only words for them. My superiors made no distinction between civilians and combatants. As far as they were concerned—and I came to believe them entirely on this point—there were only enemies in Iraq, and all Iraqis were enemies.

I know that many Americans have their minds made up about people like me. They think we are cowards who just couldn't take it. I don't blame them. I had my own mind made up about war deserters long before I set foot in Iraq. But I know right from wrong. I had a conscience by the age of six. I had to suspend it for a while in Iraq. Soldiers are taught that it is "Army first, God second, and family third." I am not a coward and I never flinched from danger. The easiest thing would have been to keep on doing what I was told to do. Ever so slowly, as

8

the jets raced and the illumination rounds burned and the houses fell during the long Iraqi nights, my conscience returned. It could no longer be Army first, God second, and family third. It had to be the tiny voice inside me that would not sleep any longer. *I am not this man,* I told myself. *I cannot do these things any longer.*

This is the story of how that voice finally grew louder than the rumbling of tanks and the blaze of gunfire and the hollering of commanders. This is the story of how it came to be that I went to Iraq as a private first class in the United States Army. This is the story of what I did to the Iraqi people and what I saw other Americans do to them, and why I deserted the war and became an outlaw in my own country. I was made to be a criminal in Iraq, but I am a criminal no longer and I am never going back.

1
Childhood

I could have used a father's advice before decid-
ing to join the army. A father could have guided me
through my worst hours in Iraq. And by the time I ran
away from the American army, I was starving for the
counsel of an older man. I wished for a father with two
basic qualities: knowledge of war and love of his son. But
there was no such man in my life. There was no one at
all who fit the bill. Anonymously, I called an army lawyer. His job was to advise soldiers in distress, but the only
thing he gave me was an earful. "Soldier," he said on the
telephone, "you've got two choices. You get back to Iraq
or you go to jail."

Hanging up the phone, I took comfort in the arms of my wife. Without Brandi, I could never have made it through the hell of living as a fugitive. I was a total mess. I couldn't sleep. Couldn't handle crowds. Couldn't even stand in a supermarket checkout line. All around me I imagined grenades launching, bullets pinging off concrete, and the heads of decapitated Iraqis accusing me of war crimes. I kept reaching for my weapon—an M-249 squad automatic weapon, thirty-six pounds fully loaded—and felt naked without it.

In Iraq I learned that every soldier has his story. One man who was ripped apart by an explosion in his armored personnel carrier told me, as I picked up his leg and put it beside him on the stretcher, "Now I get to see my daughter." Others sank under the weight of "Dear John" letters and had no reason at all to go home.

As for my own story, I am not yet thirty but feel as if I have already lived four distinct lives. In my first life, I lived at home in Guthrie, Oklahoma, and then started a family of my own with Brandi. In the second life, I spent eighteen months in military training and at war in Iraq. In the third life, I deserted the U.S. Army and hid in Philadelphia for fourteen months, slinking under the cover of darkness from one cheap hotel to the next. In this current life, I am hanging on in a new land with my wife and children, waiting to see if the Canadian courts will let us stay.

★   ★   ★

I was born in 1978 and grew up on a farm on the outskirts of Guthrie, a small town twenty miles north of Oklahoma City. The land was owned by my grandfather Elmer Porter, who bought it after serving in the Korean War. Elmer had been an airplane mechanic at Tinker Air Force Base, but he was retired by the time I came along. He lived on the property with my grandmother Doris Porter. Some aunts, uncles, and cousins of mine had their own houses on the property, and my mother, brother, and I lived in a two-bedroom trailer about two hundred yards from my grandparents' house. Before heading to school, I would often stop by my grandparents' bungalow for breakfast. Doris always made me eggs over easy, and Elmer cooked bacon in an iron skillet. My memories of eating with them are the fondest of my childhood. They were the rocks in my life, and I took refuge in their home when it was too hot or too violent in the trailer.

Doris and Elmer were Pentecostal Christians. Elmer said it was wrong for a man to hit his wife. I never saw him raise a finger against anyone. He showed me how to whittle and taught me how to fix motors, pumps, and fences on the farm. He kept ten ancient tractors that he couldn't bear to part with. Every spring, while I held his tools, he would tune them all up and drive each one around the property.

When I was thirteen or so, my grandfather said there was no room on the farm for seven new puppies. He had a quick death in mind. It was nothing to him—nothing more than avoiding a situation where he would have to feed too many dogs. I knew he didn't mean to be cruel, and I suspect he thought that with his sharp blows to the head he was bringing them an instant and painless death. But I had seen his solution before and just couldn't stand by and watch him take a hammer yet again and kill the puppies that way. So I dug one big hole in the woods behind my trailer, spread the puppies out on the ground, aimed my .22 rifle, and shot them each once at point-blank range, hoping to spare them the misery of my grandfather's hammer. I covered the pups with dirt, stood up with the shovel, took a step back, and could hear two of them still weeping under the ground. I dug them up in a panic. Two of them were barely moving, but they were still whimpering. I knew they were suffering and I didn't like to see anything suffer. I choked back the realization that I had just caused them more pain than my grandfather would have done with his own technique. I ran back to the trailer as fast as I could, opened the unlocked gun cabinet, and scoured the shelves for a weapon I knew would be loaded already and much more powerful. I grabbed a silver nine-millimeter Ruger pistol and ran back to the hole. I shot every round from the gun—I believe it was thirteen bullets—into the bodies below. My lungs were heaving, and my body was racked with sobs, and I shot indiscriminately until I knew for sure that all the puppies were dead. I didn't speak to a single person about what I had done, and for weeks I was haunted by the killing of the weeping dogs.

My grandmother Doris smoked Virginia Slims and was always crocheting, sewing, or knitting. She watched *Walker, Texas Ranger* every day on TV. She used to make pecan pies and let me eat them warm. On nights when it wasn't safe in the trailer, I slept near my grandmother in her bedroom. Doris was religious, but she swore like a trooper. She was reliable on one hand and easygoing on the other, and I loved my grandmother more than anyone else in the world.

The day before I flew from Fort Carson to Kuwait, I called Doris on the telephone. I told her that I would think of her every day while I was overseas and asked what she was doing that day.

"I'm covering all the house windows with plastic," she said.

I chuckled. "Grandma, what's all that foolishness about?"

"In case of chemical attack," she said. "Half the folks in Guthrie are doing the same thing. People say we might get chemical attacked, so they're covering up their windows."

I laughed out loud. I wished I could be there to hug the woman and fix her a glass of iced tea.

"Grandma, you ought to sit down and relax. Forget covering the windows. Plastic won't help you if we get chemical attacked. If that happens, you might as well just bend over and kiss your ass good-bye because we're all gonna die."

She laughed and said it was probably true. She said that I should take good care of myself, and that she would always love me. I never heard her voice again. Doris died seventeen days after I flew into war.

When I was still a teenager, my father almost came back for me. His name was Donald Ernest Key. I knew little about him. He had three sons from an earlier marriage, but I've met them only once. He was a welder and he drank too much. He took off when I was three and never paid my mother a cent of child support or alimony. The next time I saw him was twelve years later, when he was lying in his casket. I heard that he had died in an accident while working on an oil rig off the coast of Africa. I was told not to go to his funeral, because he had remarried and his relatives might think I was chasing his money. So I didn't go to the funeral but I went to the visitation. I spoke with his sister, who said she had heard that Dad had recently come to see me. That seemed a strange thing to say, since I had never seen or heard from him. A little later, I wandered through the woods on our property and came across a beaten-up old lawn chair in a grove of trees. Empty liquor bottles were strewn around the chair. Peering through the growth I could see my own yard. I assumed that my father had hidden himself there to watch me coming and going on school days. Who else would have been hiding in the woods on our family farm, south of Guthrie, emptying bottle after bottle of Wild Turkey? It sure wasn't my stepfather, J. W. Barker, who kept his own beer locked up in a refrigerator in his bedroom. My father was said to be a fine welder, but he never found the courage to speak to me.

My mother's name is Judy Porter. She is fifty and lives in Guthrie. She has heart trouble and a pacemaker and uses an oxygen tank to breathe. I speak to her almost every day by telephone but haven't been able to see her since I went AWOL four years ago. Most deserters get caught, and they get caught being stupid. They just can't resist the urge to visit their loved ones. It was fortunate that Brandi and the children came with me the moment I went into hiding. And it was a good thing I never went back to see my mother. The military police would have caught me for sure. Mom told me that after my desertion she saw strange cars parked down the road. Even Captain Bower, my commanding officer in Iraq, called my mother on the telephone. Bower told her that a number of soldiers had deserted his company of 120 men, and that he had caught every last one of them except for me. He warned that she could be charged if she helped me in any way. "Aiding and abetting a criminal is against the law" is the way Mom said he put it.

Here is how I avoided detection: by following every word of training that I received in the army. When your job is to defuse land mines and to set plastic explosives on people's doors before busting into their homes, you either pay attention to details or die with your head up your ass. After I went AWOL, there was one detail I never forgot: *If you don't want to get caught, don't go see your mother.*

17

Unlike the men who walked in and out of my life, my mother did not have a drinking problem. However, by the time I was in high school she rarely got out of bed or left the house. She never went to meet my teachers. She never drove to a football game to cheer me on. She hardly went anywhere at all. Looking back, I think she was depressed because she had married a string of alcoholics. Earlier, when she was healthier, she served coffee and meals at a local truck stop on the road to Oklahoma City. When I was nine, a trucker named James Willard Barker moved in with my mother and became my third stepdad. He stayed eleven years with my mother before he finally left.

I can credit J.W. with one thing: he did such awful things to my mother that I learned the hard way how not to act. Nobody deserves the kind of treatment J.W. dished out. J.W. intimidated and dominated my mother, my younger brother, and me. His reign of terror lasted until two things happened around the same time: I finally outgrew him and he developed cirrhosis of the liver.

When I was a young boy, I doted for years on a black, brown, and white weenie dog with a ridiculously long tail. His name was Buttercup and he slept in my bedroom. Not long after J.W. moved in, he made me put Buttercup outside on a cold winter night. I begged my mom to let me bring Buttercup in from the freezing weather, but she said that I had to obey my stepfather. The next day, I searched everywhere but couldn't find my dachshund. Two days later I found Buttercup huddled under the trailer, frozen to death.

J.W. got rid of my mother's animals too. She had been keeping horses, goats, and chickens for years, but J.W. sold every one of them off. Drinking money, I supposed.

It didn't take long before I hated him and wished for his death. A short, muscular man who wore a cowboy hat and cowboy boots, J.W. kept dozens of loaded weapons in unlocked cases in the trailer. I learned how to use them all.

On my ninth birthday, as a lark while his drinking buddies looked on, J.W. let me hold his nickel-plated .357 Magnum pistol.

"Go ahead," he said, "see how it feels. Pull the trigger. It's not loaded."

When I pulled the trigger, a bullet exploded from the barrel. The gun flew up and rocked my shoulder, nearly knocking me over. Witnessing my humiliation, J.W. and his buddies bent over in laughter.

I already knew how to shoot a .22 rifle before J.W. came into my life, but under his watch I learned to clean, load, and shoot every weapon in his collection. In the field behind our trailer I shot pistols, shotguns, and rifles. By the age of twelve, I was shooting M-14 and AK-47 assault rifles.

Someone gave me an Uzi around that time, and I used it to shoot snapping turtles in the pond near our farm. When I hit them, the turtles would fly up in the air and land on their backs in the water. I had a mortal fear of snakes, and one day I spotted a large one wrapped around a tree. I ran home, loaded a twelve-gauge pump-action shotgun, raced back to the tree, and blasted the sucker over and over. My grandfather, who had seen me while working outside, teased me about it for a long time. "Did you need all those rounds for just one snake?" he asked.

I began to hunt at the age of nine or ten. I didn't need a permit because I was underage. On a hunting trip a few years later, I spotted a deer two hundred yards away. Aiming a Remington seven-millimeter rifle with a scope, I shot a four-inch bullet into its neck. I felt a rush of adrenaline. When I ran up to take a closer look, I found blood everywhere. It was shocking to me. I felt horrible. The animal seemed big-eyed and defenseless, its life utterly wasted. J.W. made me help as he hung the deer from a branch and gutted it. Blood and guts spilled over our hands and arms, but we had to keep moving so the meat wouldn't spoil. It didn't matter that we ate the meat, or that it tasted good. My first deer became my last, and I did not go hunting again.

J.W. was obsessed with guns, but everybody else in the family had them too. My mother kept one by the side of her bed, and to this day my eighty-year-old grandfather packs a pistol in his pocket.

Twice in my thirteenth year I nearly shot J.W. The first time, J.W. gave me a .410 shotgun and told me to put it away in the gun cabinet. To check if it was loaded, I pointed it at the window and pulled the trigger. When the shotgun blasted, some pellets hit the fireplace and others shattered the window. I missed J.W. by about an inch. He screamed and hollered about how I was a fat, stupid, dumb-assed retard.

The second time, I heard our trailer door open in the middle of the night. I reached for my twenty-gauge shotgun, which I kept with rounds of ammunition in the bedroom that I shared with my brother, Tyler. I picked up the gun and stepped out into the corridor, pointing it forward. At the same moment, J.W. stepped out into the hall with his AK-47 pointed at me. The door had merely blown open in the wind. We saw each other just in time, lowered our weapons, and returned to our bedrooms.

Gun accidents weren't uncommon in my world. J.W. had a daughter from a previous marriage, and she had a son named Nathan. For his fourteenth birthday, Nathan received a handgun from J.W. Later, Nathan played with it in his bedroom. While looking at the barrel he pulled the trigger and blew his head off. Everybody said it was an accident. And in high school, I had a seventeen-year-old friend named Chris Coleman who died at a party when someone put a nine-millimeter pistol to his head and pulled the trigger. Then too, the kids at the party assumed it was not loaded.

J.W. bossed me around and called me stupid and fat all the time, but he reserved the very worst for my mother. When J.W. got drunk, something evil came over him, and he went looking for her.

Once, Mom got up from the dinner table and opened the dishwasher to reach for a plate. Without provocation, J.W. swept up behind her, grabbed the dishwasher door, and slammed it shut against her hand. Mom let out a scream and went to hide in her room. She never wanted us to see her when she was in pain. Mom went to the doctor a few days later, claimed she had fallen down some stairs, and came home in a cast. I wished that the doctor had paid a house call. Surely he would have seen that there were no stairs in our trailer. Maybe he would have demanded another explanation for the broken hand.

Another time, J.W. loaded Tyler and me into his car and raced up to the highway restaurant where Mom was working. As soon as he barged through the door he began shouting that Mom had been sleeping with other men.

Mom stared at him, eyes wide. "Are you crazy?" she said. "Go away. I'm working."

But J.W. would not stop shouting. Finally, the boss came out and told my mom to leave. She lost her job. Mom drove back home in another car, and I rode with her while she cried and said she had no idea what J.W. had been talking about. I remember seeing him punch her when we got back home. After that, my mother stayed in bed most of the time, depressed and unable to do anything for herself or for us.

I wasn't yet eleven.

After Mom lost her job, the troubles continued. Alone in our bedroom, Tyler and I could feel the trailer shaking. We knew it was Mom, being thrown against the walls. I looked out through a crack in the door and saw J.W. rip a phone off the wall and use it to smash my mother in the head. I came out of my room and saw blood running from her ear. J.W. hollered at me to get back and to close the door behind me. Mom, too, pleaded with me to stay out of it. She went to the hospital and came home with a bandage like a turban around her head. J.W. had broken her eardrum.

Sometimes in the morning I would notice a scratch or a bruise on J.W.'s face. That would make me light up in a moment of private victory. The battle scars meant that my mother had managed to scratch or punch back at least once during the beating. I could not understand why she wouldn't leave him, and I could not believe that his brothers would just sit around and drink beer and watch without a word of protest when J.W. beat my mother.

I wonder if seeing my mother get beaten up so many times led me to feel, in the end, that it was only normal that I, too, should have a few knocks in life. When I was sixteen, I began my first part-time job. A few evenings a week, I worked in the Kentucky Fried Chicken outlet in Guthrie for about $5 an hour. One day, while I was changing an oil filter on a deep fryer, I accidentally placed my hand in vegetable oil that was boiling in a vat. The grease exploded against my face and one hand. I jumped back and leaned over a sink to throw water over my face and hand. I could feel that I had been seriously burned, so I asked the manager to call an ambulance. She was busy serving customers and refused to help me. I ran out the back door to my truck to drive myself to the hospital. The truck had a flat tire. With blistering hands and a face that felt like it was on fire, I had to change the flat before I could jump behind the steering wheel and drive with my third-degree burns to the hospital. I never returned to work at Kentucky Fried Chicken, but I didn't stop to think that I deserved better treatment and never even thought about making a complaint.

Somehow, I survived my childhood. Perhaps it helped to feel normal and to know that other people had it much worse. Maybe they didn't have enough food to eat. Maybe their loved ones were sitting in prison. Maybe a man named Timothy McVeigh had just blown up their folks in Oklahoma City. It was probably just as well that I didn't know that my own life was difficult.

I wouldn't wish my childhood on anyone, and I want to protect my own children from a life like mine. But I will say one thing for it: learning to cope day after day with harshness gave me the strength to push through the nightmare in Iraq and the stubbornness to find a way out. Perhaps my childhood outrage rekindled after some months in Iraq and made it possible for me to do the one thing a soldier must never do: think for myself and question my commanders.

The Oklahoma summers were hotter than hell. My brother and cousins and I would make mud pies and watch them dry out in the sun. It never took long in 115 degree heat. My cousins liked to swim in the pond, but I mostly stayed out of the water because I lived in fear of cottonmouth snakes. We dug pretend war tunnels underground and shot paint balls at one another until, at thirteen, we graduated to whiskey and beer and racing down country roads in pickup trucks.

We called the spring "beer-drinking weather," and early on we found two more ways to amuse ourselves. After drinking late into the night we would go out cowtipping in farmers' fields. Cows fall asleep standing on their feet, and we would sneak up and knock them over real fast. They had no balance at all and would topple like bowling pins. Farmers didn't like our pranks, and we had to clear out as fast as we could before someone caught sight of our license plates.

Our second amusement was mailbox crashing. A friend and I would go tearing down the road in my 1992 Nissan pickup. While he drove, I leaned out the side window with a baseball bat, swinging at the country mailboxes. You can get in a decent pop at thirty miles an hour.

Three miles down the road lived my junior high school shop teacher. Mr. Smith was a heavyset man with gray hair and Coke-bottle eyeglasses. He wasn't a bad teacher, but he had an irresistible mailbox. Each time I smashed up his mailbox he put in a new one. Finally, he installed a rubber mailbox. The baseball bat didn't do any good, so I—using a recipe from *The Anarchist Cookbook*—cooked up homemade napalm on my friend's kitchen stove, carried it in an old paint can, and poured it all over the mailbox, which melted. Once more, my shop teacher couldn't get his letters delivered.

Some of the men in my life—my grandfather and J.W. in particular—had a lot of prejudices about blacks and Asians. One time, I was working in a doughnut store run by one of my aunts and my grandfather happened to be there when a number of black college students walked through the door. I was mortified to hear him mumble aloud about how he wished the Ku Klux Klan would come back. I noticed one of the students giving him a withering look, as if to say, "You are one pathetic loser." I was relieved that he and his buddies got out the door without incident and—even though I loved my grandfather deeply—resolved not to be like him in that respect. I brought black friends by the house, and kept doing it even after he asked me to stop. "Grandpa, you've got to get out of the 1950s," I would tell him. "It's the 1990s now."

I think that the fear of the unknown—blacks and Asians, in this case—led my grandfather to hold those prejudices, and I would say that the very same fears made it easy for too many American soldiers—myself included— to abuse Iraqi civilians. In our training, our commanders taught us to demonize and hate Iraqis and Muslims. Looking back, I am sorry to admit that some of the negative parts of my own upbringing climbed from the darkness of my soul and shook hands, in a way, with my army training. It took some time in Iraq before I could put the hateful thoughts behind me.

During my childhood in Guthrie, folks used to say that one day there would be another war between the North and the South. People sometimes wish they could bring back the past, but I don't think they truly want war in their own backyards. If they had any idea of what war meant—if they could picture blood spilling from white, black, or any other bodies—I am quite sure they wouldn't want it. I learned this the hard way, at war in Iraq. The first time an innocent civilian died before my eyes, I didn't ask myself questions about her racial or ethnic background. The only question to ask was why she had to die in the first place. When I look back at my childhood in Guthrie, I think all the talk about bringing back another war between the North and the South was just a way to let out hot air, and no more than an ignorant way to shoot the breeze. I think that deep down all such people really wanted was to pass the time by watching—or joining in—an old-fashioned fistfight. The summers were hot and god-awful boring, and there wasn't much to do in Guthrie except get drunk and start fighting. In that respect, I quickly became a model citizen.

I got in my first fight when I was eight. A thirteen-year-old boy started picking on a kid in my grade, so I kicked the bully in the face. He was a foot taller and a whole lot bigger. He blacked both of my eyes and busted my lip. I had another stepdad back then, and I feared that I would get a whupping for coming home beaten in a fight. I had been at a football game, and when my stepdad came to pick me up I pointed out the boy I had fought. My stepdad noticed the size of the older boy and said I had done enough for the day.

I fought through junior high and kept fighting in high school. I fought black kids and I fought white. I even fought teammates on my football team. I fought so many times that my jaw still locks up on occasion from having taken so many punches.

When I was about seventeen, I got arrested for taking a swing at a police officer who tried to stop me from going to help my mother during a forest fire. My grandmother nearly got herself charged for barging into the police station, swearing at all the officers, and demanding my release.

In court, the judge suspended the charges when he heard that the police officer had ganged up with other cops and roughed me up. My only requirement was to attend a few classes on anger management. I took the classes with two men who had gotten into all sorts of trouble. One of them had beaten up his ex-wife's boyfriend. Not long after the anger management instruction ended, I discovered the two classmates yet again pounding the snot out of the ex-wife's boyfriend. At the time, I thought that anger management was a bit of a joke. Looking back, however, I think that everybody would have been better off if a few soldiers I know had been sent to anger management class instead of Iraq.

★ ★ ★

These days, Brandi and I don't let our children play with toy guns. I see the irony in that. Zackary, our eldest, is nine years old. When I was his age, one of my favorite pastimes was to stand alone in the backyard, blasting apart beer bottles with a .22 rifle. Because he'd come from another country, had an American accent, and took some time fitting into his new Canadian school, Zackary became the target of a bully. One of my biggest challenges as a father was *not* to tell him to cock his arm and slug the bully in the mouth. But I know that Zackary will do better things in life and that the world will be a better place if he learns to use words to solve his problems.

My first experience with terrorism was in my home state of Oklahoma, and I know that 168 lives would not have been lost if a man named Timothy McVeigh had been taught to use words instead of force. In 1995, when the ex-soldier and war veteran blew up the federal building in Oklahoma City, we felt the blast in our high school some twenty miles away. McVeigh used a truckload of ammonium nitrate—cow shit fertilizer, basically—to kill all those people, including nineteen children. A boy in my school lost his dad in the explosion, and a girl lost both of her parents. Before the explosion, some of the kids in school had teased this girl about coming from a poor family. The teasing stopped after the explosion. I had no idea what to say to a person who had lost both her parents, so I just felt sorry for her and said nothing at all. Classes were canceled as soon as we got the news. We assembled in school for the rest of the day to watch the television reports.

Within forty-eight hours, the police had charged Timothy McVeigh with blowing up the building. I couldn't believe it. I had figured it was the work of a foreign terrorist. But it was an American—a former gunnery sergeant in the 1st Infantry Division in the Persian Gulf War—who had blown up his own people.

When I started going out with Brandi, she knew that I had gotten into my share of fights down by the Cimarron River, but her background was just as rough as mine. She had plenty of fights under her own belt and had also been warned that she'd face consequences at home if she lost a fight in the streets. I told her I had seen my mother get beaten too much, and that I would never beat a woman. She liked that about me. She liked everything about me. She was so like me that there was barely anything that needed explanation. We were both poor, had grown up with way too much violence in our family lives, and wanted to put the worst of our lives behind us. I knew, within five seconds of meeting her, that she wanted to be a good person and to lead a good life. I believe she felt the same way about me.

Brandi and I were both eighteen when we met. I was still in twelfth grade but she had already graduated from high school and was working in a dollar store. The day after we met, I stopped by the store to ask her out to dinner. She accepted the date but persuaded me to forget the restaurant and settle on fast food. Why waste money when we could park the pickup by a quiet creek, talk, look out at the water, and let the night grow late?

Brandi liked my mother, but she could read J.W. like a book. She knew the score. When Brandi was three her mother was murdered. At the time, her father had been doing a seven-year jail term. J.W. tried to tell Brandi and me what we could and couldn't do in bed, but we didn't listen to him. It wasn't his trailer anyway, it was my mother's. To hell with his instructions that Brandi sleep on one side of a bedsheet and that I sleep on the other.

Although I tried to have as little as possible to do with J.W., I liked his father a little better. His name was Bill Church, and he had fought in the Korean War. He had been sprayed with tear gas in Korea and lost an eye. I tried to ask him about Korea, but he never wanted to talk about it. The last time I spoke to him was just before leaving for Iraq. He cried to hear the news that I was going to war. He said he understood that I had to go but warned me to be careful.

I have seventeen cousins and various aunts and uncles and Brandi has relatives too, but we have hardly spoken to any of them since I deserted the army. With the exception of my mother and my brother, most of them are scandalized by what we have done. I believe they fear they'll have trouble with the law if they talk to us, and so have written us out of the family. Brandi and I lost more than just our country when we came with our children across the border at Niagara Falls, New York. We lost our families too.

★ ★ ★

Brandi and I agree that it was love at first sight. We were inseparable from the day we met. Within two weeks we made plans to get married. We wanted to have a decent wedding, but we couldn't save enough to pay for it.

Brandi and I took an apartment together after I graduated from high school. We worked at every imaginable kind of job. Wherever we went, Brandi worked as a waitress and I held down jobs as a welder, general laborer, roofer, cook, salesperson, or pizza delivery man. I usually made about $7 or $8 an hour. We moved all the time in search of better jobs and better pay. When things got too hard in Guthrie, we tried our luck in Oklahoma City. Then we tried Madison, Wisconsin. And then we moved back to Oklahoma City.

Zackary, the first of our children, arrived in 1998 when we were both twenty. In February 1999, Brandi and I gave up on our dreams for a family wedding and eloped to Arkansas. We were married by a justice of the peace. We had a crowd of four: Zackary, Brandi's sister, and her father and stepmother. Brandi's folks took care of Zackary during our one-night honeymoon. We stayed in a hotel in Muskogee, Oklahoma, and ordered in pizza for dinner.

By the time Adam came along in October 1999, Brandi and I were finding it hard to live on her tips and my salary. Changing cities and jobs never led to better pay. I picked up some welding work on a few of the jobs but got no formal training. To cut down on costs, we bought clothes at secondhand stores and stayed in run-down apartments. Our place in Oklahoma City had holes in the floor and in the windows. The water didn't run and the toilet didn't work. The place didn't even have a stove. Brandi had to go to her grandmother's home to cook for us.

Brandi had Oklahoma state health insurance for herself and our children, but I had no health insurance. One day, I felt stabbing pains in my back and started urinating blood. I drove to a hospital in Oklahoma City, but they turned me down because I had no insurance. The next hospital I tried let me in and X-rayed the kidney stone but couldn't get it out. In that first of four hospital visits for kidney stone problems I was billed more than $2,000. I couldn't pay it. Our debts piled up while our credit rating sank. I still have the stone in me and it still acts up.

By the year 2000, when we were both twenty-two, Brandi and I had become desperate. With two young boys, we didn't even have money to see the dentist. Our families were too poor to help much, but Brandi's grandmother sometimes gave us food. We never had as much as $50 in the bank. When we were living in Wisconsin, Brandi and I started talking about the military as a way to get out of poverty. I tried to enlist in the U.S. Marines, but they turned me down because I had two children and too many debts.

Brandi and I managed to keep going. By 2002 we were back in Oklahoma City. Brandi was looking after Zackary and Adam, and Philip—our third child—was on the way. I had a job delivering pizza and was allowed to take home as much as I wanted for dinner. We got sick of pizza awfully fast. I decided to try my luck once more with the military. This time I would try the army. Maybe their standards wouldn't be as high. In March, I drove to the U.S. Army recruiting station in Moore, Oklahoma. At last, I found some good luck. Or so I thought.

2

Recruitment and Training

I HAD DRIVEN PAST IT MANY TIMES BEFORE. THE U.S. armed services recruiting station was located in a strip mall in Moore, a suburb of Oklahoma City, not far from where Interstate 240 meets Penn Street.

I didn't dress up to make an impression on that first day in the recruiting station. I felt better in my T-shirt and jeans. I had only ten dollars in my pocket—just enough for milk and cigarettes—and Brandi had forty dollars at home, and that just about summed up our life savings on that day. So even if I had wanted to dress up, there was no money for it.

Outside the recruiting station someone had plastered posters promoting life in the armed forces. Every

35

word of those posters seemed designed for people like me. I had no money, I had dreams of getting formal training as a welder, I needed to get my teeth fixed, and I wanted to have my kidney stone removed. If I only joined the military, the posters suggested, I would be on easy street. The armed forces were offering money for college tuition, health insurance, and even a cash bonus for signing up. To top it all off, military service would give me a chance to travel and discover a new way of life.

Brandi and I didn't like being in Oklahoma, and we wanted to get out. For folks like us who were poor and getting poorer by the day, the posters suggested that getting a job with the armed forces would be like winning the lottery. The difference, of course, was that almost nobody wins the lottery. But just about anybody can get into the armed forces—unless he or she is as poor as I was. It had been humiliating to be booted out of the marine recruiting center, two years earlier, because of my debts and growing family. This time, I would have to be honest about my situation, but I sure hoped they would take me.

When I walked in I saw recruiters behind six desks. I walked up to a staff sergeant whose name was something along the lines of Van Houten.

He was a tall white man, heavyset, and he looked like he was in his late twenties or early thirties.

"I'm thinking of joining the army," I said.

Van Houten stood up and shook my hand.

"What's your name?"

"Joshua Key."

"Can I call you Josh?"

I grinned. "Everybody does."

"Good Oklahoma boy, are you? Me too. Grew up not far from here." He did have an Oklahoma accent. He pointed to a chair. "Sit down, son, and make yourself comfortable. Hungry? Thirsty? We've got lots of stuff around here."

"No thank you, I'm fine."

"Well, how about just coffee then?"

"All right, coffee would be good."

"What do you take in it?"

"One milk and five sugars."

"You like a drop of caffeine with your sugar, do you?"

I grinned again. He called for someone to get me a coffee, just the way I had asked for it, and within a minute the steaming cup was sitting in my hand.

Van Houten had a stack of papers on his desk and a pen in his hand.

"All right with you if I ask a few questions?" he said.

"Sure."

"That's good," he said. "'Cause I have a lot of them."

"Fine with me."

Van Houten began with the basics. What was my full name? Where did I live? Where and when was I born? What were the names of my father and mother, and where and when were they born? What was my education? Was I married? How many kids did I have?

I told him everything, but Van Houten slowed down a bit when we got to my family situation.

"What is your wife's name?"

"Brandi Key."

"Maiden name?"

"Johnson."

"And your kids?"

I told him about Zackary and Adam and said we had a third child on the way.

He raised one finger, stopped me right there, and spoke in a low, confidential tone.

"All right, not another word about your wife being pregnant, is that understood? We leave that part out. You can't enlist if you've got three children, but if everything else checks out I can get you in if we leave that part out."

"Okay," I said.

"And whatever you do," he said, "don't mention it to the commanding officer here." Van Houten offered to swing by my home to speak to Brandi about all the family benefits associated with life in the military, but he warned me to keep Brandi away from the recruiting station so that no superior military officers would notice her pregnancy. I got the message loud and clear.

Van Houten told me to keep one or two other details to myself as well. He would not take down information about the two herniated disks from an early back injury, because he said that could complicate my entry into military life. He didn't want me to say anything about the time I had been arrested for assaulting a police officer. When I began to raise the matter of my debts, which had made it impossible for me to join the marines, he stopped me once more. "I won't ask and don't you tell," he said.

Van Houten gave me the impression that, as a favor to me, he was leaving out all the details that might hurt my chances of getting into the military. He became my coach, my guidance counselor, my adviser, and my personal biographer, as well as the provider of coffee, doughnuts, and submarine sandwiches over the next five or six weeks.

I had imagined that it would be possible to apply, be tested and checked out, and sign up in a day or two, but the process stretched out for the better part of six weeks.

After completing the initial questionnaire, Van Houten told me to return at five-thirty in the morning a few days later to take an aptitude test.

"Have a good meal, get a good night's sleep, and eat breakfast before you come in for the test," he said. "You'll do better that way."

I showed up on time and spent two hours on a question-and-answer test dealing with math, English, mechanical understanding, and general knowledge.

There were about thirty young men and women in the room, and we all got our scores as soon as we finished the test. I was told that 30 was the passing score and that

99 was the highest score possible. I got a 49, then saw to my amazement that not a single other person in the room had passed the test.

Van Houten told me that 49 was a good score, but that if I wanted I could take the test one more time to see if I could get a 50, which would give me more choices about where to go in the military. I took the test again but got the same score.

One of Van Houten's colleagues, a short, thin, middle-aged government employee in civilian clothes named Daniel Russell, told me that I had three options. I could become an infantryman, a multiple-launch rocket systems driver, or a bridge builder.

"Can I join the army without having to go overseas?" I asked. "I don't want to leave Brandi and the kids."

"Absolutely," Russell said. "I can give you the bridge-building position in the continental United States. That means right here on the continent. You wouldn't even have to go to Hawaii or Alaska."

"Bridge builder sounds good to me."

Russell leaned forward over his desk and looked into my eyes. "I can get you a seven-thousand-dollar signing bonus if you pick one of the other two options."

I asked for more details. Russell explained that working as an infantryman or as a multiple-launch rocket systems driver would involve combat duty. I made it clear to him that I did not want to leave my country or go into combat.

"Think about it," he said. "Seven thousand dollars."

"I don't have to think anymore on that one, sir. I don't want to do combat duty. Not even for seven thousand dollars. Tell me more about bridge building."

Russell told me that the army employed many men to fix bridges in the continental United States. I would not receive any signing bonus, but the advantage was that I would be allowed to choose to go to a "nondeployable" military base. "Nondeployable," Russell explained, meant it was a base that did not send men to war.

When I pressed for more information, Russell said that if I wanted to do bridge building, the closest military base was at Fort Carson, Colorado. I told him I had never heard of it. Russell explained that Fort Carson was in Colorado Springs and was home to a military unit called the 43rd Combat Engineer Company.

"But that sounds like combat," I said.

"It sounds like that, but it isn't what you think," Russell said. "It's a nondeployable base, and you will be put to work building bridges in the United States. It's called Combat Engineer because you have to blow up bridges, sometimes, before you can build new ones."

"So this means I can stay with my family and don't have to go overseas?" I asked again.

"Soldier, it will be as easy as cheesecake. You're going to be building bridges from nine to five every day and spending every evening at home with your family."

It sounded too good to be true. But Russell promised to write "CONUS," short for "Continental United States," right on my contract if it would help put my mind at ease.

Our conversation ended there, and I felt a little more relaxed about my future in the army.

A week or two after I first showed up at the recruiting center, Van Houten came to my home and immediately won Brandi over. Life on the military base was secure, he said. We wouldn't have to worry about violent criminals breaking into our home and hurting our children. We would stay in clean, decent accommodations that any working American would be proud of, he said. The rent would be free on base. (I learned later that this was not true, that about $700 would be docked every month from my paycheck for the rent.)

The whole family would have access to comprehensive health insurance, he said, and I would be able to get up to $20,000 in tuition for college studies. I told Van Houten that I wanted to get training as a welder, and he said the money could be used for that, and that I could even begin college studies while posted to my military base.

Over the next several weeks I had to see Van Houten nearly every day to take additional tests and to fill in more paperwork. Every time I came into the recruiting station he offered me something to eat. What is more, he offered to take me along when he went jogging or did weight training in the gym of nearby Tinker Air Force Base. I accepted, joining him some thirty times at the gym. On each trip, he bought me coffee and a sandwich. Van Houten offered up a little information about himself. He was married and had three children and came from Lawton, Oklahoma. He was looking forward to returning to his regular military job as a surveyor at Fort Sill, Oklahoma, but for the time being he was stuck recruiting young Americans and working on a quota system. I can't remember exactly how many men he said he was required to recruit, but I believe it was about one person per week. He was stressed out about it and said he couldn't wait to return to his former job as a military surveyor.

"They rip up my ass if I don't make my quota," Van Houten said.

For my medical and physical tests, I peed in a cup, gave blood, and was made to walk like a duck—knees bent and squatting low with my butt near the ground. I asked about that and was told the test would indicate if I was flat-footed. Apparently, you could not get into the military with flat feet. It seemed that they gave me every vaccination known to mankind, including eight shots against anthrax.

I was almost twenty-four when I applied, and I felt old compared to the bulk of the applicants, who appeared to be teenagers. Young men and women who were just seventeen were allowed to join if they had permission from their parents. I would say that about three-quarters of the applicants were men and one-quarter were women.

One day, a teenage girl entered the recruiting station and began to apply for entry to the army. A little later, a lieutenant colonel in military apparel burst through the door. All the soldiers and noncommissioned officers in the room jumped to their feet to salute him. Somebody whispered to me that he was in the marines. He swept by us all, grabbed his daughter by the arm, and shouted for all of us to hear, "There is no goddamn way that any daughter of mine is joining the fucking army." He dragged her out the door and that was the last I saw of her. I had heard that marines and soldiers hated each other, but this was the first time I saw the emotion expressed openly.

Another time, at a military entrance processing station—a separate building to which I often had to go as my application inched forward in the army bureaucracy—I saw a poster on a wall that read: "Desertion in the time of war means death by a firing squad."

I watched a young man and woman standing under the poster.

"Oh my God," she said, "can they really do that?"

I wondered the same thing as I was made to sign a paper saying that I had read and understood the poster.

Finally, in mid-April 2002—just a month shy of my twenty-fourth birthday—I learned from Van Houten that the army had cleared all of my medical tests and paperwork. I was fit to join the United States Army, he said, and I would do my country proud. He explained that I would receive $1,200 a month in salary and commit to a three-year contract. He did not tell me what I would learn only later—that the army could recall me anytime it wanted up to seven years after I signed up.

One last time, before signing, I asked Van Houten for reassurance that I would not be sent into combat and that I would be allowed to live with my family and work for the army in the United States.

"If World War Three breaks out and they are sending everybody overseas, then you could be required to do duty as well," he said. "But even then, it would be unlikely. Because of your growing family, you would be the last person to be sent overseas."

That seemed reasonable to me.

To seal the deal, Staff Sergeant Van Houten looked me in the eye, man to man, shook my hand, and said, "Soldier, you ain't got anything to worry about. You're going to be building bridges in the continental United States and home with your family every evening."

Two other noncommissioned officers looked over my shoulder, turned the pages of the contract, skipped over the fine print, and pointed out all the X's where I was to sign my name. I signed where they pointed and believed what I was told. I was a bloody fool to do so.

On April 13, 2002, I entered into a contract with the U.S. Army. Eighteen days later I was sent to basic training in Fort Leonard Wood, Missouri.

★　★　★

I took a commercial flight from Oklahoma City to St. Louis. At the airport, I met up with about 150 other new recruits. We boarded a number of military buses. It was a long drive to Fort Leonard Wood, but at least I was on the military payroll now. Brandi—who went to live with our boys in Checotah, Oklahoma—would be able to buy the children some clothing, and we would all eat a little better.

We pulled into the fort around three a.m. As we prepared to disembark, a long line of drill sergeants awaited us. They shouted that we had to get off the bus immediately, screamed that we were worthless assholes, and hollered that anything could be changed in the contracts we had signed and any promises made to us could now be thrown out the window.

The drill sergeants held megaphones as we all scrambled to get out. "Get the fuck out!" they screamed right in our faces.

Like the others, I was nervous and scared, but I knew—even amid all the pushing and the shouting—that they were just trying to break us down mentally, and that more of this would come.

We had to give up our cigarettes, lighters, scissors, and nail files. We were taken to the barracks, allowed to sleep for an hour, then rushed to a mess hall and given one minute to eat. And I mean one minute. I wolfed down the scrambled eggs as fast as I could.

A day after our arrival I was allowed to call Brandi. I had only a minute or two on the telephone with her, and

I wouldn't be given another chance to call her for seventeen weeks. Quickly, I told her that they did not let us have coffee or tea in boot camp and that she should send me some over-the-counter uppers called Yellow Jackets. You can't get them any longer but back then they were perfectly legal, and you could buy them at any gas station or drugstore in Oklahoma.

Ever the dutiful wife, Brandi slipped the Yellow Jackets inside a box of Zest soap, repackaged the bar of soap, and sent me the uppers by mail. Every morning I swallowed a pill to jolt myself awake.

Within a day or two of arriving at Fort Leonard Wood, while I stood at attention with three hundred other recruits, a drill sergeant hollered out that we had been put into the 35th Combat Engineer Company and that we would learn to be "the most devious goddamn killers on the battlefield."

I didn't know exactly what that meant, but it sure didn't sound like bridge building. I tried not to worry about it because I still believed that after boot camp I would be sent to a nondeployable military base. So, to my way of thinking, it did not matter if I learned about grenades and mines because I wouldn't have to use them in combat anyway.

I turned twenty-four just a few days after arriving at boot camp. I didn't tell anybody, because I didn't want to draw any attention to myself. If anybody notices you or stops to speak to you at boot camp, it's bad news for sure. The name of the game is to stay out of sight of anybody in any position to rain down punishment. When sergeants blew horns and banged trash cans at two in the morning, hauled us out of bed and made us each do a hundred push-ups, I tried to struggle through it and to stay under the radar.

I shared a bunk bed with a private named Babbit, who was steaming over a lie he had swallowed during recruitment. The poor sucker had been told a story like mine—but even more ridiculous. A recruiter in Lawrence, Kansas, had promised Babbit that if he signed up for service, the army would reward him and his girlfriend with a holiday to Korea. When Babbit got to Fort Leonard Wood and found out that his Korean junket had disappeared about as fast as my bridge-building promise, his girlfriend dumped him.

"When I get back home I'm going to find that recruiter and tell him that he's a lying piece of shit," Babbit fumed.

Among the three hundred recruits, about a third of us were white, another third black, and another third Latino. There were just two women. As we went through the seventeen weeks of basic training, we were all shouted at, insulted, awoken abruptly, and kept off balance by sergeants whose job it was to break us down and build us back up in their own mold.

If somebody failed to do something properly, every recruit in the company would be punished. That quickly taught us to hate laggards and people who just couldn't follow orders quickly enough.

I must say that I loved boot camp. I was good with guns, didn't mind the exercise, and felt myself swell with patriotism and pride when our commanders told us that Americans were the only decent people on the planet and that Muslims and terrorists all deserved to die.

One day, all three hundred of us lined up on the bayonet range, each facing a life-size dummy that we were told to imagine was a Muslim man.

As we stabbed the dummies with our bayonets, one of our commanders stood on a podium and shouted into a microphone: "Kill! Kill! Kill the sand niggers!"

We, too, were made to shout out "Kill the sand niggers" as we stabbed the heads, then the hearts, and then slashed the throats of our imaginary victims.

While we shouted and stabbed, drill sergeants walked among us to make sure that we were all shouting. It seemed that the full effect of the lesson would be lost on us unless we shouted out the words of hate as we mutilated our enemies.

I shouted as loud and stabbed as mercilessly as any man on the range, and I slowly began to feel that I was somebody important. I was no longer a fast-food delivery man earning a pittance for a wage plus tips and all the pizza I could eat. I was no longer wondering how I could possibly put enough food on the table for Brandi and the boys. I was now an American soldier, and proud to think of myself as a perfect killing machine. I felt patriotic and invincible. I believed every word I was told, including that it was the job of the American army to keep order in the world. Our commanders told us that people who were not Americans were "terrorists" and "slant eyes." They said that Muslims were responsible for the September 11, 2001, attacks on our country, that the people of Afghanistan were "terrorist pieces of shit that all deserved to die."

Commanders drilled these beliefs into us by making us memorize and call out various chants. I have trouble remembering the precise words of all of these chants, but one of them went something like this:

> *One shot*
> *One kill*
> *One Arab*
> *One Asian*

Another of our chants had to do with putting our skills as sappers, or makers and defusers of bombs, to good use:

> *Who can take a shopping mall*
> *And fill it full of people?*
> *The sapper daddy can,*
> *'Cause he takes a lot of pains*
> *And makes the hurt go good.*
>
> *Who can take all the people in the mall*
> *And chop 'em up with Uzis?*
> *The sapper daddy can,*

'Cause he takes a lot of pains
And makes the hurt go good.

Iraqis, in the mouths of the officers and soldiers of the United States Army, were never Iraqis. And Muslims were never civilians. Nobody once mentioned the word "civilian" in the same breath as "Iraq" when I trained to become a soldier. Iraqis, I was taught to believe, were not civilians; they were not even people. We had our own terms for them. Our commanders called them ragheads, so we did the same. We called them *habibs*. We called them sand niggers. We called them hajjis; it wasn't until I was sent to war that a man in Iraq explained to me that hajji was a complimentary term for a Muslim who had made the pilgrimage to Mecca. In training, all I knew was that a hajji was someone to be despised. The hajjis, habibs, ragheads, and sand niggers were the enemy, and they were not to be thought of with a shred of humanity. No wonder my wife and I both thought, by the time I flew overseas to war, that all Muslims were terrorists and all terrorists were Muslims and that the only solution was to kill as many Iraqis as possible.

There is one other thing I was taught at Fort Leonard Wood that chipped away at my soul and made it that much easier, a year or so later, for me to accept and take part in the violence that my fellow soldiers dished out to civilians in Iraq.

Twice during my time at boot camp, a drill sergeant by the name of Johnson made me get up from my bed in the middle of the night, collect one or two aides, and beat up recruits who were falling behind in their duties or failing to comply with orders.

Sergeants, I was told, were not allowed to beat up trainees. So they used me to do their dirty work, and I, stupidly, felt honored to do exactly as they said.

The first time, Sergeant Johnson sent me to beat up a trainee named Taylor, who had lunged at a drill sergeant and tried to start a fight with him. My buddies and I threw a blanket over his head and beat his chest and ribs with a sock stuffed with soap. I whacked him hard while he cried out in pain. "You been making trouble for all of us and there will be more of this tomorrow if you keep it up," I said.

After taking his licks, Taylor didn't try to start any more fights with noncommissioned officers.

A little while later, Sergeant Johnson sent me out again, to beat up a recruit by the name of Armstrong who had been refusing to take orders. Once more, my buddies and I jumped on him in the night, covered his head, and pummeled his body. Armstrong screamed during the whole beating and kept on screaming when we left. I had to run back and threaten to beat him again if he didn't shut up. He fell silent after that, but in the morning I saw that my intimidation tactics had not worked.

When we were awakened in the morning, Armstrong began shouting to anyone who would listen that he would not get out of bed and that he would not follow orders. The drill sergeants took him away, and I never saw him again. I heard that he was let out of the army, although I don't know if that is true. At the time, I thought of him as a weakling and a coward who was an embarrassment to the army.

I enjoyed boot camp. I liked the challenge involved in setting and defusing land mines. It was fun to learn how to set off bombs using plastic explosives and TNT. One day, well into our training, we were rewarded for our hard work with the opportunity to set off a bomb consisting of about two hundred pounds of C-4 explosives. After hiding inside a bunker at a distance of a few hundred yards, we ignited the bomb. The blast roared in our ears, and the earth shook. I felt the vibrations rolling through my body. Dirt and debris flew through the air. I had never witnessed such a powerful explosion in my life, found the experience exhilarating, and hoped I would get to make another bomb and see it explode.

I loved shooting on the practice range, and I earned a pin for my good marksmanship. When we were tested in rigging and defusing bombs, I got top grades in my company. After nine weeks of basic training, five weeks of sapper training, and three more weeks of training in how to drive tanks and armored personnel carriers, I moved to my permanent military station at Fort Carson, Colorado.

In October 2002, Brandi, the boys, and I moved into a modest row house on the new base. I still believed that Fort Carson was a "nondeployable" base, one that did not send soldiers to war, but that last bubble burst within minutes of my arrival.

A specialist named Abby was sent to pick me up at the reception area on base. When he showed up, he said that I would be joining the 43rd Combat Engineer Company.

"Since the nineteenth century, we've been in every major war the United States has fought and we're proud of it," he said.

I was shocked, but I said nothing as he drove me to my barracks.

Over the next days, I learned that I had been placed in the third squad of the first platoon of the 43rd CEC, as it was called. Each squad had six or seven members, so there were about twenty people in a platoon. There were six platoons in the 43rd CEC, for a total of about 120 men. Most of us were combat engineers, trained in how to make and defuse bombs and mines. Our company was part of the second squadron of the 3rd Armored Cavalry Regiment. The 3rd ACR had its own distinguished wartime history. Known also as the "Brave Rifles," soldiers with the 3rd ACR's precursors had fought in the American Civil War, the Spanish-American War, both world wars, and the Persian Gulf War, among others. One of the 3rd ACR's most famous and colorful generals was George S. Patton Jr., who during World War II favored ivory-handled Colt .45 revolvers and traveled with a bull terrier named Willie.

Shortly after arriving at Fort Carson, I paid a visit one afternoon to the office of Lieutenant Joyce and found him sitting in his chair.

"Do I have permission to speak, sir?"

"Yes, soldier."

"Sir, when I joined the military I was told I was being sent to a nondeployable base. But I hear that the 43rd Combat Engineer Company is a combat company. Is there some way we can fix this problem, so I can be sent to a nondeployable unit?"

"Soldier, you obviously don't understand the military way of life. Get the hell out of my office."

I felt that everything was lost, and that I should get out of his office before I made matters worse for myself. I paid for that complaint.

The next morning my squad leader, Sergeant Padilla, shouted in my face.

"You broke rank by speaking to Lieutenant Joyce and you're a fucking piece of shit."

The team leader at the time, Specialist Abby, continued with the endless stream of insults. I was "smoked," as they say, for several days. They made me do push-ups, duck walks, crawl around on my hands and knees, and stand at attention while every man in my platoon hollered that I was a "useless asshole" and a "stupid shit."

We have an expression in the army: Drink water, drive on. It means that when things get bad, you just have to suck it up and keep going. When I learned that I was in a combat-ready army company and that I might be sent to war at any point, I believed I had no choice but to take it and keep going. I felt humiliated to be taking abuse from every man in my platoon. I wanted to fit in and be respected. I wanted, one day, to be promoted to the rank of sergeant. I wanted them to see how fast and steady I was with my hands. Whether it came to shooting rifles, planting bombs, defusing mines, or driving trucks, I knew that I had fantastic hands and sensed that the only way to earn their respect was to show them how good I really was. I could put a mine in the ground and take it back out within a minute or so.

Sure enough, the abuse and insults continued until we were out on a demonstration range a week or two after my arrival in Fort Carson. The fall weather had turned cold and we were using a heater to stay warm in the field. But the heater stopped working. After I fixed the alternator and restored heat for my platoon buddies, I earned the name MacGyver—after the inventive television character—and was never called a "shit bag" again. I drank water and drove on.

I could never quite follow my instructions to rank the army first, God second, and family third in my own personal priorities, but I did my best to fit in and prove myself in the six months that passed before we were told to say good-bye to our families and pack our bags for war.

3

Early Days in Iraq

I BELIEVED THE REASONS THAT PRESIDENT GEORGE W. Bush gave for beginning the Iraq War on March 20, 2003. I had faith in my country and accepted what I was told: Iraq was stockpiling weapons of mass destruction and harboring terrorists behind the 9/11 attacks on the United States. I accepted the argument that it was time to overthrow Saddam Hussein and bring democracy to Iraq. I wasn't eager to fight, but I would follow my commanders. As I've stated, I thought it was better for me to help stomp out terrorism and defend America than to leave the job to my own children.

When Operation Iraqi Freedom began, I was a private first class in the U.S. Army, stationed in Fort Carson,

Colorado, with the 43rd Combat Engineer Company. Although our tanks and other military equipment had been shipped to the Middle East long before the offensive began, I suspected that we might not be sent into action. Soldiers in my platoon talked all the time about how, in the Persian Gulf War in 1991, it had taken the American ground offensive only one hundred hours to drive the Iraqis out of Kuwait.

Sergeant Padilla, one of the noncommissioned officers in my squad, said not to worry about going to war. He said he had gone to the first Persian Gulf War, but then had simply waited for months in the Arabian desert, far from combat at all times. It would probably be more of the same this time, he told me.

I gave my wife similar reassurances. "It will be over before they can lift our butts into the air," I told Brandi.

But Padilla and I were both wrong. On April 10, just three weeks after the American offensive began, I left for war with my company. We flew from Colorado Springs to Frankfurt, Germany, and then to Kuwait. I barely slept on the flights and kept wondering what I would be doing in Iraq. I expected I'd be using my military training in explosives, clearing the Iraqi desert of land mines so that American tanks could roll safely by. Leaving the plane in Kuwait, we boarded buses on the tarmac. En route to the military camp, I couldn't keep my eyes from drifting to the television screen on the bus. *Teletubbies*

was playing—in Arabic. This was the first of many sur-
prises during my time in the Middle East.

We stayed about two weeks at Camp Illinois in the
Kuwaiti desert. We were rationed to one MRE (Meal
Ready to Eat) and one liter of water per day, but Sergeant
Lindsay—who was in charge of my platoon—ordered us
to steal water left at night outside tents belonging to other
army companies. I wondered about the surprise and anger
that would break out among the soldiers who woke up to
discover that they had no water in the desert. But as a private first class, I was on the bottom of the chain of command and anxious to prove myself. I took the water
without getting caught. Shortly thereafter, Lindsay gave
me a similar order. At night, when others were sleeping, I
was to steal lights from other companies. Once more, I
managed to do it without getting caught. After stealing
them, I hooked up the lights to generators so that we could
see inside our own tents at night.

During our time in the camp, I was sent to Kuwait
City to help unload Abrams tanks from ships and get them
lined up on flatbed trucks to be taken across the desert. I
was excited to see a bit of the city—especially all the people
driving Ferraris and Lamborghinis—and I got carried
away while driving the tanks. In a stupid moment, I tried
spinning a tank around in a circle, just to feel how well it
maneuvered. In so doing I crashed into another tank. An
air force officer saw the crash, but she then looked the
other way. Luckily for me, the last thing she wanted was

to be dragged into writing accident reports. I got away from there as fast as I could, walking with one hand on my chest—directly over my name and rank—so that I couldn't be identified and disciplined later.

On April 27, we packed up our things at Camp Illinois and began a fourteen-hour journey across the desert to Iraq. Our long convoy consisted of hundreds of flatbed trucks carrying about one thousand men from various military companies, as well as Humvees, Abrams tanks, and armored personnel carriers (APCs). We moved at a snail's pace—about twenty miles per hour. I sat up with one of the truck drivers, and along the way looked out at blown-up tanks and discarded vehicles with bones strewn about them.

Somewhere inside Iraq, our convoy divided into smaller pieces. Our company of 120 men was sent alone into Ramadi. It would be our job to relieve the 82nd Airborne Division and to take control of the city of some 300,000 people. I was terrified and expected that we would be driving straight into a war zone. I imagined Iraqi soldiers launching grenades and spraying bullets, and it didn't seem possible to me that such a small group of Americans could defend themselves in the city. However, on entering Ramadi, we were greeted with waves and cheers. Children racing up toward our vehicles shouted for food and water. So far, at least, this was the last thing I'd expected from a war zone.

I traveled with my six squad mates in our armored personnel carrier. It was about the length of a four-door car and the width of a lane of traffic. Made of steel, it lacked the thickness of a tank and the durability to resist rocket-propelled grenades. There was room for four or so men below, and for another two or three up top to operate machine guns. From the moment I entered Iraq, I was obsessed with the thought of being caught inside a burning tank. I preferred to sit on top of the vehicle and risk sniper fire. In Iraq, whenever I traveled on our APC, I always took my position on top, monitoring the streets and the rooftops with my M-249 automatic weapon ready. The M-249 weighs thirty-six pounds fully loaded. It is formally called a squad automatic weapon, but we called it a SAW for short, because—at two thousand rounds a minute—it would saw right through any person it hit.

I was scared out of my wits that first day in Ramadi. Our own air force had just finished bombing these people, but as soon as we got out of our vehicles we began patrolling their streets, on foot. With nearly a hundred pounds of weaponry, equipment, and clothing on my back, I was about as mobile as a cow. It was just my platoon, twenty guys, walking single file through streets full of Iraqis. I could not stop thinking that anywhere, at any time, some half-starved sniper on a roof could have taken me out in no time flat. Iraqi kids surrounded me in swarms, hands out, asking for water and food.

I kept hearing the last words Brandi said to me before I flew out of Colorado Springs: "Don't you let those terrorists near you, Josh. Even if they are kids. Get them before they get you." I also kept thinking about my officers' repeated warnings: "If you feel threatened, kill first and ask questions later." I had army chants buzzing through my head, too, those chants we'd picked up in Fort Carson while we learned the ins and outs of blowing things up with C-4 explosives.

> *Take a playground*
> *Fill it full of kids.*
> *Drop on some napalm*
> *And barbecue some ribs.*

On that first day in Ramadi, when I saw kids coming at us from every direction with noses running and hands outstretched, I felt surrounded by Muslims, terrorists, bomb throwers, and killers. They came in all sizes, of that I was sure. Why not children too?

In Ramadi, my platoon set up camp in a bombed-out palace just a stone's throw from the Euphrates River. There was marble everywhere: the floors, walls, and pillars. I saw a destroyed elevator and a tiled mural of Saddam Hussein. The former groundskeeper ran up to us and said the palace had once belonged to Saddam Hussein himself. He was an older man who didn't appear to have anything to do, or any work to keep him going. He stayed near our troops to run errands and fetch drinks for the sergeants, for what I presumed was a little pocket change. I unrolled my sleeping bag on the floor, about one hundred feet from an unexploded U.S. bomb that sat half-buried in the floor, sticking out about six feet. It didn't seem like a safe place to be, but at least I had a roof over my head.

I ate my ration—beef enchilada—and tried to smother the flavor with Tabasco sauce. Most of the other soldiers had no interest in the one-ounce shots of hot sauce that came with their MREs, so I scooped them up and used double and triple doses every time I ate. Oklahoma isn't far from Mexico, and an Oklahoma boy needs his hot sauce. Sometimes, in the boredom and fatigue of life in Iraq, hoarding and gulping down Tabasco sauce became a diversion in itself. I remember still being hungry when I went to sleep that first night in Ramadi. There were no bombs dropping or mortars falling, but I was awakened at three a.m. and told to get my ass up quickly because in one hour we were going to raid a house full of terrorists.

We had a few minutes of orientation on the grounds of the palace. Captain Conde and some sergeants showed me and my squad mates a satellite photo of a house and a drawing of the layout of the inside. Our assignment was to blow off the door, burst into the house, raid it fast and raid it good—looking for contraband, caches of weapons, and signs of terrorists or terrorist activity, then rounding up the men and getting out of there damn fast. The longer we stayed in any one location, the longer somebody would have to put us in the sights of a rocket-propelled grenade or lob mortars at us.

I had no idea what to expect. Would I charge through the door, only to be blown to bits by a grenade?

Would somebody with an AK-47 knock my Oklahoman ass right back out that door? Would some six-year-old terrorist with two days of gun training be waiting to put me in his crosshairs? The minutes ticked on, and I wanted the hour to speed forward so we could get to our destination and get on with it.

One or two of the guys did push-ups to pump themselves up. I borrowed Specialist Mason's portable CD player and bombed out my eardrums to the beat of Ozzy Osbourne. It got me going. High and ready for action. I topped that up by knocking back one or two more bottles of Tabasco sauce, which gave me a nice jolt. In Iraq, Tabasco sauce became my wake-up call.

I checked my watch, wished it would accelerate, and stuck some dip—Copenhagen, bourbon flavor—behind my lip. You can't manage a cigarette when you've got an M-249 automatic weapon on your arm. So dip was best. Makes your mouth black as sin, and rots the roots right out of your gums, but dip was my nicotine hit of choice going into that raid.

I committed our preraid instructions to memory. I knew the angles of the house, what door I would help blow down, how many floors were in the house, and who would do what when we busted inside. I would be third in the door, which means I was the second most likely to get shot if anybody had a mind to take us down, and I'd head to the left. Always, for every raid, I would be third in, heading left. I gripped my M-249. Yes, it could belt out two thousand rounds a minute but only in theory. You couldn't really hold your finger down that long. When you were blazing away like that, the bullets turned the barrel as hot as Hades. And if you held your finger down too long, it would warp the barrel.

It was time to go. We went out into the cool Iraqi night. We took a civilian vehicle—a white Toyota truck—so that the Iraqis would not suspect we were coming. Sergeant Fadinetz was at the wheel. He had a map with exact directions, including information about where to park the truck. Also in the truck was our squad leader, Sergeant Padilla, as well as Sergeant Jones, Specialist Sykora, another grunt, and me. We had our basic moves plotted out, like a set play in football. We drove into an upscale Iraqi neighborhood, passed a mosque, and parked near an attractive three-story house.

We ran out. It took thirty seconds for Jones and me to put the charge of C-4 plastic explosive on the door. Then we dashed around to the side of the house so we wouldn't blow ourselves up. You wouldn't want to be standing anywhere near that door when we blew it in. You'd be fried meat if you were near the explosion. I set off the blast, and then the six of us charged into the house. Jones went first—that skinny, red-haired Ohio boy was always hot to trot. Next went Fadinetz. Then me. After me came Padilla, and then Sykora, who gobbled up professional wrestling like it was going out of style—that, and porn videos; even in Iraq, the man got his hands on porn videos regularly. After Sykora came the other grunt from our squad. It was either Specialist Mason or Private First Class

Lewis—I can't remember which of them was with me on that first raid.

With Jones leading the way we burst into the house. We were armed to the hilt. Kevlar helmets, flak jackets, machine guns, combat boots, the whole nine yards.

I'd never been inside an Iraqi's house before. We charged through a kitchen. I had been told by squad leader Padilla to check everything, so I even opened the fridge. Perhaps, I thought, I would find guns or grenades hidden inside. No such luck. In the fridge, all I saw was a bit of food. In the freezer I found big slabs of meat, uncovered. No wrapping. No plastic. Frozen, just like that. We ran into a living room with long couches, one along each wall. In this room with the abundance of couches we found two children, a teenager, and a woman. We also found two young men in the house. One looked like a teenager and the other was perhaps in his early twenties—brothers.

We hollered and cussed. I spat dip on the floor and screamed along with the other soldiers at the top of my lungs. I knew they didn't understand, but I hollered anyway.

"Get down," I shouted. "Get the fuck down. Shut the fuck up."

They didn't know what "get down" meant, so we knocked the two brothers to the floor, facedown. We put our knees on their backs, pulled their hands behind them, and faster than you can bat an eye we zipcuffed them. Zipcuffs are plastic handcuffs that lock on tight. They must have bit something fierce into those young men's skin. There was no key, nothing—the only way to get them off was to slice them with cutters.

We pushed the brothers outside, where twelve other soldiers from our platoon were waiting. Some loaded the Iraqi men onto the back of a truck. Others were "pulling perimeter," which meant keeping guard to make sure that nobody entered or left the house or the surrounding area.

The Iraqi brothers were taken away to an American detention facility for interrogation. I don't know what it was called, and I don't know where it was. All I know is that we sent away every man—pretty well every male over five feet tall—that we found in our house raids, and I never saw one of them return to the neighborhoods we patrolled regularly.

Inside, we kept on ransacking the house. The more obvious it became that we would find no weapons or contraband, the more we kicked the stuffing out of the house. We knocked over dressers, sliced into mattresses with knives, kicked our way through doors, raiding the three bedrooms on the second floor, then raced up to the third floor. Would we find terrorists or nasty weapons stashed there? Nope. It was basically just a landing that led to a rooftop area where the family had washed clothes and hung them to dry.

We turned over everything we could and broke furniture at random, searching for contraband, weapons, proof of terrorist activity, or signs of weapons of mass destruction. We found nothing but a compact disc. Soldiers initially said it showed proof of terrorist activity, but it turned out to have nothing on it but a bunch of speeches by Saddam Hussein.

I figured the terrorists had managed to dance out of our way that night, but that we'd nab them the next time.

Once we had everybody outside the house and had done our initial job of ransacking, another squad took over inside. They kept raising hell in there, breaking and turning over more furniture, looking for weapons that we might have missed. Outside, under a carport—a parking space under a roof, but with no walls or enclosure—I was assigned to watch the women and children. We weren't arresting them, but we weren't allowing them to go anywhere either. The family members couldn't go back inside, and they couldn't wander off into the neighborhood. They had to stay right there while we tore the hell out of their house.

A girl in the family—a teenager—started staring at me. I tried to ignore her. Then she began speaking to me. Inside, when we had been screaming at her and the others, I'd assumed that nobody understood a word of English. But this young girl spoke to me in English, and her eyes bored holes right through me. She was skin and bones, not even a hundred pounds, not yet a full-grown woman, but something about her seemed powerful and disturbing.

I feared that girl, and I wanted to get away from her as fast as I could, but it was my job to stay right there and make sure she didn't move. I had my weapon ready. She was wearing a blue nightgown and had a white scarf covering her hair. She had no veil, so I could see her face perfectly. Her eyes were coal black and full of hatred.

In English, she asked me, "Where are you taking my brothers?"

"I don't know, Miss," I said.

"Why are you taking them away?"

"I'm afraid I can't say."

"When are you bringing them back?"

"Couldn't tell you that either."

"Why are you doing this to us?"

I couldn't answer that.

I hoped she would not raise a fuss. I didn't want her to start screaming, which could attract the attention of my squad mates. One or two of them, I feared, would be more than happy to use a rifle butt to knock out her teeth.

I hadn't been in Iraq more than twenty-four hours and already I was having strange feelings. First, I was vulnerable, and I didn't like it. Even with all these soldiers and all this equipment, I knew that anywhere, at any time, any enterprising Iraqi with a gun, a wall to hide behind, and one decent eye could pick me off faster than a hawk nabs a mouse. Second, with hardly one foot into the war in Iraq, I was also uneasy about what we were doing there. Something was amiss. We hadn't found anything in this girl's house, but we had busted it up pretty well in thirty minutes and had taken away her brothers. Inside, another squad was still ransacking the house. I didn't enjoy being stuck guarding this girl under the carport, in the cool April air before dawn in Ramadi. Her questions haunted me, and I didn't like not being able to answer them—even to myself.

I dared not speak more with her because that would amount to "fraternizing with the enemy"—something about which I would be warned many times in Iraq.

In the days to come I tried to drive that girl out of my mind. We hadn't found a thing in her house except slabs of meat in the freezer and a Saddam Hussein CD. No matter. We'd catch the terrorists the next day, to be sure. Or so I told myself.

We were pumped after that raid. It felt like a pouch of adrenaline was slung on an IV and dripping straight into my veins. It was one of the most exciting things I had ever done. After the first hit I wanted more. I wanted to catch those fucking terrorists, and I figured it was only bad luck that had prevented us from nabbing them the first time.

We were told that the purpose of the house raids was to nab terrorists and to find evidence of terrorism. During that first month in Ramadi, we usually raided at least one home— and sometimes as many as four—each night. The houses we raided were ordinary, one- or two-story homes in residential areas. They were far more attractive, spacious, and comfortable than the trailer, apartments, and houses I had inhabited in Oklahoma. Most of the houses in Iraq looked neat, tidy, and well arranged—before we showed up. Our raids always took place in the middle of the night, in order to catch people sleeping and to intimidate them.

My whole platoon, consisting of about twenty officers and soldiers, would take part in the house raids. Twelve or so soldiers would place themselves outside, six positioned as guards and another six stationed at the trucks used to take away all the men—or any boys over five feet tall—that we found inside. It was always the job of my squad of six or seven men to begin the raid itself. I was usually the one to put the plastic explosives on the door, set the charge, and blow down the door. I never saw a person killed in a house raid, but if any Iraqi had been standing just inside his front door at the moment I blew it off, he certainly would have been killed.

When we burst in the door, sometimes we raced through the house and found people in bed. At other times men and women were standing or sitting inside, looking completely stunned. Sometimes their hands would fly to their mouths. Sometimes they would start screaming. We would scream at them to get down and knock down the men as quickly as we could so they could be zipcuffed and taken out to our waiting trucks. Any male who took his time about getting to the floor or who protested loudly would be given a quick rifle butt to the head or the stomach. I dished out my fair share of licks in those first raids.

Although I lived in terror in the first month or two that somebody would ambush us in the midst of a house raid—throwing grenades or lighting us up with machine-gun fire—nobody ever resisted with as much as a finger.

Looking back, with twelve American soldiers stationed outside and six more charging into the house, each one armed to the hilt and ready to shoot, I can see that resistance would have been suicide for any Iraqi. Even though not one person tried to shoot us or made any effort to hurt us, it was common for American soldiers to beat the civilians. At least every two or three days during my time in Iraq, I saw our soldiers kicking Iraqi civilians in the ribs and punching their faces until blood ran from their noses, mouths, or eyebrows. I'm not proud to say that I participated in these beatings, but I was far less extreme than some of the soldiers. As time went on I lost any appetite for the beatings and refrained from them entirely.

We got the men outside as fast as we could, and it usually took longer to round up the women and children. The women would sometimes scream at us, and we would shout right back at them to "shut the fuck up." Sometimes they spoke English and sometimes they didn't. Often, we had no idea what they were saying and the only language of ours they understood were our pointed machine guns.

Inside the houses, we knocked over wardrobes, kicked in doors, ripped through mattresses, and threw bookshelves to the floor. We busted locks, threw over refrigerators, and broke lanterns and lamps. Radios and televisions were thrown around and smashed.

In the first raid, the second, the third, and the fourth, I wondered why we never managed to find anything. We tore the hell out of those places, blasting apart doors, ripping up mattresses, breaking locks off furniture, and ripping drawers from dressers. With all of our ransacking, we never found anything other than the ordinary goods that ordinary people keep in their houses.

We commonly found AK-47s in the course of our raids—just as commonly as one might expect to find guns in houses in Guthrie, Oklahoma—and we didn't consider this unusual or evidence of terrorism. Initially, we confiscated every weapon we found. But after several weeks, Sergeant Padilla told us to stop taking them because Iraqis used them for their personal protection. Each family could keep one AK-47, Padilla told us. At the time, I thought that was perfectly ludicrous. I couldn't see the point of raiding houses if we allowed the very people who were supposed to be our enemies to continue to own automatic rifles. During my entire stay in Iraq, the rules about whether or not to take AK-47s from houses kept changing. One week, we would be told to take every assault rifle we found. A little later, we would be instructed to let families keep a weapon for personal protection. Over time, I expected to find one gun in each house and paid it no more attention than I would a television.

Other than weapons and people, the only things we found in our house raids were books, clothes, rugs, furniture, and food. When we found money, jewelry, or knives, we helped ourselves to them and to anything else that caught our fancy.

Not long into my stay in Iraq, I saw $100 in a house. I snapped up the bills and stuffed them in my pocket. A man who was being zipcuffed and led out the door shouted back at me angrily.

"Why are you taking that money? It's not yours."

"This is American money," I told him. "You're not American, and you have no business having it." The money stayed in my pocket.

Jewelry. Money. If it looked good, we helped ourselves.

I stole whatever I wanted in the initial raids, but I stopped doing that after my first few weeks in Iraq. The more uneasy I felt about what we were doing there, the less I wanted to make matters worse. Others in my platoon looted to their hearts' content. One fellow collected gold jewelry and mailed it home to his wife. Another lugged a television straight out of an Iraqi house. Others took ornate knives, and I saw one soldier make off with a beautiful rug. Who was going to stop us? We were the army of the United States of America, and we would do whatever we pleased.

I still believed that eventually we would find the terrorists or the weapons that were said to be there, but it didn't take long before the raids left me feeling uncomfortable. It was easy to see the hatred in the eyes of the Iraqis as we broke apart their houses and arrested their men.

In the raids, I came to dislike the way Sergeant Jones loved to be the first one to bust into the homes. Jones, a freckled man from Ohio, had already done war duty in Afghanistan. He was just twenty-two, and I resented the fact that a man two years my junior outranked me in the squad. He had no wife or kids. He had been in the U.S. Army for years and talked about staying in it forever. One of the things that upset me about Jones was what he had said to me in Fort Carson, Colorado, the day before we flew into war. He wanted to get my goat and he knew exactly how to mess me up. "It's a known fact that your wife is gonna start fucking some other guy the moment you're out of the country. You wait. You'll see. It happens to them all. By the time you're back, she will have stolen your money, served you divorce papers, and found herself another man." I loved my wife to bits. Brandi and I already had three children, and I had never doubted her. But the seed of anxiety that Jones planted grew like a weed during my time in Iraq.

I thought of Brandi and of our children when Jones and I charged into civilians' houses. Jones had no family, but I did, and it tore me apart to terrorize families like that. We were finding no weapons of mass destruction or evidence of terrorism. I soon began to feel that breaking apart a house and terrorizing its inhabitants was not something that should be done to any human being. Period.

One of the things that disturbed me the most in the house raids was having to run into bedrooms and round up sleeping Iraqi children. I couldn't help imagining how my own children would react if armed soldiers from another country burst into their rooms and tore them from bed. I was supposed to keep my guns trained on the children when I woke them, got them out of bed, and marched them outside. I couldn't do it, though. I could never point my M-249 at a child. I would tap the children gently on the shoulder and the poor kids would leap from bed, petrified, screaming like the world was ending. And outside they would go, as their brothers and fathers were being zipcuffed and shoved onto the backs of trucks and sent out to who knows where.

Our first month in Ramadi—from the last days of April to about the end of May 2003—was the quietest and easiest of my time in Iraq. The people of Ramadi had been bombed before our arrival, so perhaps it took the Iraqi resistance some time to get organized. During our first tour of duty in Ramadi, we were not subjected to rocket or mortar attacks, nobody launched grenades at us, and almost nobody took shots at us as we moved about the city. Nobody in my platoon was injured or killed. I fell into a pattern of four basic jobs: raiding homes; patrolling streets and traffic checkpoints; standing guard at banks, hospitals, and military compounds; and doing grunt work where we had put up camp in Saddam Hussein's bombed-out palace.

Even back at the palace we never got much sleep. Apache helicopters hovered and jets screamed above us at all times. At night, our forces shot constant illumination rounds into the sky. The rounds were like giant firecrackers, exploding one after the other so that darkness was never allowed to settle over Ramadi. Sometimes I was ordered to patrol the banks of the Euphrates, located just a stone's throw from the palace. I would often see Iraqi fishermen in small boats, pulling the pins out of grenades and tossing them into the river. They would wait for the water to stop gushing up in fountains, and then they would scoop up all the dead fish. Eating fish full of shrapnel didn't seem like much of a meal to me, but the men were desperate for food and a livelihood.

I ran a pipe from the Euphrates to our palace and rigged up a pump so that the men in our platoon could use a makeshift shower. I also connected our electrical wires to the Iraqi power grid so that our lights, fans, and air conditioners could run. I could have been electrocuted at any time, but I never stopped to worry about the dangers. I was living in constant fear of being attacked, was jacked up on adrenaline from all of the house raids, and was never allowed to sleep more than a couple of hours at a time. As a result I felt constantly stoned, and didn't think any more about the juice in the Iraqi power grid than I did about sleeping next to an American bomb or wandering out in the middle of the night to urinate next to an unexploded rocket-propelled grenade.

Because I was among the lowest-ranked, I got stuck every few days with one of the worst jobs going: to burn up all of our shit. We crapped into fifty-gallon metal barrels, each sliced in half. When the barrels were full, I would toss in five gallons of diesel, light a match, and use a fence post to stir the shit. Usually I would have two or three barrels burning at once, stirring them for hours at a time. I would have to keep tossing on more diesel and lighting more matches, and I had to keep stirring to make the shit burn. As I worked, the ashes settled all over my face and my hands. It took hours to burn down our shit that way. In the first platoon of the 43rd Combat Engineer Company I became the main shit burner, and I imagine I stirred more of it than any soldier in Iraq.

During our quiet time, some of the men read or listened to music. Most of them played Game Boys. Many times, we gathered together in groups to watch bootleg videos that we purchased from Iraqi street vendors or from Sayeed, a nineteen-year-old Iraqi who had studied in England and who was paid $20 a week to serve as our interpreter and errand boy. On portable DVD players, we watched every kind of film imaginable. Action films. War movies. Porn. One time, Sayeed brought us a porn movie featuring Asian children. While I watched in horror, a teenage girl in the video was tied on a stretcher and raped by two men. In the middle of a war zone, with tanks rolling and jets screaming, I stared numbly at the screen and asked myself what had gone wrong with the world. The other soldiers and I sat there stupidly and watched until Staff Sergeant Lindsay broke up the show, called us all perverts, snatched the DVD, and broke it with his hands.

Our commanders told us it was okay to masturbate, because they wanted us to check if we had any blood in our sperm—which, we were told, might suggest that we had ingested *E. coli*. For a laugh, some of the men began a competition to see which one could go the longest without masturbating. We worked on the honor system, but it would have been hard to lie anyway.

Because I was eating with, crapping next to, sleeping beside, and busting into homes with the same guys day in and day out, I ended up knowing them all pretty well. There's barely a thing about them I didn't know. I knew whose wife has just written him a Dear John letter or, worse, told the poor guy, after he had stood in line for two hours to use a phone, that she had a new man in her bed. I knew who came from Indiana and who hailed from Alaska. I knew who liked video games and who read Dean Koontz novels. I knew which soldier had the biggest penis —measured by socket wrench, while the rest of us looked on—and who wanted to take a course in small engine repair when he got the hell out of Iraq. But one thing I almost never knew were the guys' first names. We all had our last names written on our uniforms, and our rank clearly marked, so we all went by our last names. Nobody knew me as Josh. Nobody called me Josh. I was Key to one and all of them, and I knew only their last names.

Because I grew up on a farm in Oklahoma and because I was five foot nine and weighed 215 pounds, I got called "fat boy" more times than I care to remember, and I had to listen to a whole lot of nonsense about how people from Oklahoma fucked hogs. My weight dropped fast in Iraq, however, and people stopped teasing me when they realized I was the quickest guy around when it came to using my hands. I can make just about any broken thing work. I may not fix it properly, but I'll fix it well enough to make it go again, and as a result they started calling me MacGyver again. Under orders, I jump-started Iraqi trucks, taxis, and cars. By making myself useful, I kept the bullshit off my back and I managed to get along with most soldiers.

Specialist Sykora got it into his head to ask Sayeed, our interpreter, about how to make sexual taunts in Arabic. He and a bunch of others learned to say something like *sofeeni deeaytcha,* which was supposed to mean "show me your tits," and *sofeeni goose goose,* which apparently meant "show me your pussy." On foot patrols he and a few others would shout the words at Iraqi women in the street. I never said those words, and I worried about the safety of the Iraqi women. Sometimes they were walking with their husbands. If their situation at home was anything like my mother's, I knew that their husbands would beat them just for having been taunted in this manner.

One day, while we were guarding the children's hospital in Ramadi, Jones—who also enjoyed taunting Iraqi women—stopped a woman doctor as she was entering the building. He made her remove her veil. I told Jones to leave her alone, but it was too late. She removed the veil and stared into Jones's face. In her eyes I could see liquid fury. Later that day, as she was leaving, she passed us again and said to Jones, "Actually, you asshole, I was born and raised in Boise, Idaho." She went on to say that she had come to Iraq to help her people during the war. Jones was so embarrassed that he could not speak, and I was pleased for the woman from Idaho.

In the month of May, my platoon was ordered to go to the Ramadi police station to retrieve a truck full of rocket-propelled grenades and mortars. I was told that the truck contained one thousand rounds of live ammunition that had been taken from the Iraqis in battle. Escorted by our platoon, Iraqi police officers drove the truck full of ammunition to an isolated spot fifteen minutes outside the city, but we were ordered to wait for authorization before blowing up the truck. In a display of typical army inefficiency, we left the truck unguarded in the desert and returned to Ramadi. The next day, after receiving the detonation order, we returned to blow up the truck. But it was gone. I shook my head in disgust. *Great work,* I thought. We just gave a thousand rounds of ammunition right back to the enemy.

After about a month in Iraq, the 43rd CEC was transferred out of Ramadi. We moved to Fallujah for a two-week period. One day in early June, not long into our stay in the new city, my platoon mates and I were standing guard outside a public building. Local Iraqi officials met in this building and held talks there with our own military commanders.

While standing at the back of the compound, I felt the ground shaking under a good thirty seconds of heavy gunfire. The barrage came from the other side of the building, which was being guarded by members of the 82nd Airborne Division. I heard voices crackling on army radios.

"What happened?" my squad leader asked.

"Looks like somebody got trigger-happy," someone else said on the radio.

It was clear that once one soldier had started shooting, everybody else had joined in. A few minutes later, I saw about a dozen body bags being carried away and was told that the victims were all Iraqi civilians. It was the first time I was aware of Iraqi civilians being killed by American soldiers. I heard no more about the incident. I was struck by the absence of discussion in the aftermath. I kept my mouth shut. Soldiers were not allowed to ask questions; to do so showed insubordination and invited punishment. In my presence, no soldiers or officers asked how or why the civilians had been killed, and no explanations were offered. I came to see that silence usually followed in the wake of a killing.

One of my jobs in Fallujah and elsewhere was to monitor cars at traffic control points. We stopped cars, searched them, and searched drivers. When we found people out driving after the nighttime curfew, we detained them and took their vehicles.

I hated it when people smiled at me at checkpoints. It made me want to punch them. What did they have to smile about? Did they know something I didn't know? Were they planning some sort of attack?

Early in my stay in Fallujah, while I was on checkpoint duty, one driver got out of his car and told me—in English—to go fuck myself. I felt an explosion of hatred and anger in that moment. I started beating the man. I was even tempted to shoot him. Something about all my pent-up anger and fear craved an explosion of violence in that very moment, but Lindsay—the sergeant first class who was overseeing our platoon at the time—grabbed me and pulled me back.

"Lay off him, Key" was all he said.

He didn't punish me or say anything more about it. I was angry at the time, but not many minutes passed before I felt thankful that I had been stopped from seriously harming or killing the man.

I backed away from beating people at checkpoints but saw that others continued to hand out beatings just as often as they felt the urge.

While we were still doing traffic control in the first week of June in Fallujah, I saw Sergeant Lindsay join up with Specialist Mason to beat the daylights out of a man. My mouth fell open. Even Lindsay was losing it now. I saw the beating but had no idea what had provoked it. Maybe the man had said the wrong thing, or had smiled the wrong way. One thing was clear: he hadn't attempted any sort of assault or attack. In my countless days at traffic control points, I never once saw an Iraqi civilian threaten or harm an American soldier. Lindsay and Mason kicked the man in the back and the head and kept on kicking once he fell down. They rubbed his face in the sand and then began spitting on him. I remember thinking that it was going way too far, but I knew I didn't have the rank to stop the attack. Finally, an Abrams tank belonging to another platoon stopped and a sergeant jumped out.

"What the hell are you doing?" the sergeant asked, telling Mason to get away from the man and to stand behind the tank.

Lindsay told the sergeant to mind his own business. "My troops will do whatever I tell them to do," he said.

The tank sergeant did not outrank Lindsay, so he got back inside and drove on. Lindsay and Mason did not return to their beating, however. They let the man get up, climb into his car, and drive away. We never discussed the incident in our platoon. It was not that far out of the ordinary. Every day or two, I saw American troops beating the daylights out of Iraqi civilians. In our own platoon, all we had to do was look at our highest-ranking sergeant to see that it was okay to kick and punch Iraqis whenever we felt the urge. Fortunately, I no longer felt the urge. But I also knew that I was powerless to stop Sergeant Lindsay from punching an Iraqi civilian. If I had spoken directly to him about the beating, I would have been violating the chain of command. I wasn't even authorized to speak to a superior officer unless he addressed me first. If I saw something that concerned me in Lindsay's behavior, the only course of action—apart from keeping my mouth shut—would have been to speak to my team leader, who, if he felt like it, would have had to speak to his squad leader, who, in turn—if so inclined—would have had to go to Lindsay himself. For all that, I was sure, I would have been bawled out for leaving my post and likely docked some of my pay. The simplest thing to do was keep my mouth shut and stay out of trouble, so that is what I did.

The people of Fallujah were so accustomed to bullets flying that some of them walked about oblivious to the dangers. It was as if they felt their lives were so entirely in the hands of God that they believed it would be useless even to bother ducking for cover. One day, I was with my squad mates on our armored personnel carrier, chasing a truck. Somebody said that shots had been fired at us from the truck. As it drove and we gave chase over a bridge, my squad leader—Sergeant Padilla—sat on top of our APC, blasting away with his .50-caliber machine gun. Perched as usual on top of our vehicle, I could see an old man walking toward us. Bullets whistled past him, blasting chips out of concrete walls on the side of the bridge, but the old man kept walking calmly, as if in a dream. I thought it was a miracle that he was not hit, but he didn't even appear to be thinking about it.

Unfortunately, the violence meted out by American troops was not limited to kicking and punching. One day in our first week in Fallujah, my entire platoon—three squads, consisting of a total of about twenty men—was stationed at a traffic control point. Lieutenant Joyce was the highest-ranking officer with us that day. While the other two squads monitored approaching cars, I was busy with my squad mates searching vehicles and drivers. While I was looking under the hood of a car, checking for bombs and hidden weapons, the ground started to shake. I dropped to my knees but realized that it was fire from my own troops. The hail of gunfire came from M-16 rifles, M-249s, and .50-caliber machine guns. The fire was coming from the first and second squads of my platoon. Even a Bradley tank belonging to the 3rd Armored Cavalry Regiment (but not to my 43rd CEC) got into the act. The tank and the other squads were all firing at a white car with yellow stripes that had two people inside.

I noticed that the car had driven too close to the checkpoint, about ten feet past the line at which it was supposed to stop. As a result, it had been brought to a halt in the most murderous way. When the car stopped inching forward and the gunfire ceased, my squad mates and I ran to the vehicle. We found it riddled with bullet holes, each two inches or more in diameter. Inside the car, one man was dead. His head was attached to his neck by only a few threads of flesh, and blood was splattered all over him and the car. Nobody touched him. But then I saw a boy in the front seat. He looked like he was about ten years old. A medic pulled him out. One of the boy's arms was nearly severed, but he was alive. The boy was conscious, and he was looking at his father. With the help of the medic we put the boy in our APC, raced him to the Ramadi hospital, and dropped him off there. When we got back to the checkpoint, I spent ten minutes searching the vehicle and patting down the dead man. There were no weapons inside it. There was nothing unusual in the car, except all the blood that we had made run.

About twenty minutes later, Lieutenant Joyce got off his army radio and told us all to pack up and leave. We left the car and the driver right where they were, in the middle of the busy road. I couldn't stop thinking about how we didn't even put the man in a body bag and take him to the hospital or to our compound, where his family would know to find him. When we got back to our compound I got off my armored personnel carrier, walked behind a building, and vomited. I saw Sykora throw up too, and I heard at least one other soldier in my squad vomiting at the same time. I had never before seen a man shot to death. As far as I could tell, he was killed simply because he hadn't known where to stop his car.

The next day, as I was stationed on top of our moving APC, I looked out at the spot where the man had been killed. He and his car were gone.

In Fallujah, we stayed in a compound of bungalows located outside the city. In my own mind I called it Dreamland; its artificial lake seemed utterly removed from our day-to-day activities at war in Iraq. In our free time, we tried to forget our troubles and the shooting we had seen by jumping off a sixty-foot bridge, straight into the water. Lewis didn't want to jump, so we just pushed him off the side of the bridge. Even Sykora, who could barely swim, was forced into the water, and I watched as he dog-paddled back to shore.

Just a few days after we had left the dead man in his bullet-ridden car, the violence began again.

After nightfall our platoon left Dreamland to drive across Fallujah to a traffic control point. I rode as usual on top of the APC, holding my M-249 rifle. One of my sergeants sat up on top with me, positioned to shoot from his turreted

.50-caliber machine gun. Specialist Mason was driving. Two APCs belonging to the other squads were directly ahead of us and behind us traveled an Abrams tank.

As we approached an intersection, I saw a small white pickup truck driving in our direction. It looked like a Toyota or a Nissan. It made a quick left-hand turn, cutting in front of us. This split us off from the second APC, but I saw no sign of danger and there were about thirty yards to spare. Nonetheless, my sergeant let loose with his .50-caliber machine gun. Blasting away with bullets about six inches long, he shot the car and brought it to a halt. I saw a trail of gas leaking from the car. The sergeant shifted his gun, aimed at the trail of gas, and shot again. The line of gas caught fire and flew back toward the truck, and when it hit the gas tank the truck exploded in a ball of fire.

We kept on driving. I looked back at the explosion and the fire. I watched our Abrams tank roll right through it and keep following us. It looked like something straight out of *Rambo*. The boys in my squad let out some hollers of delight.

"Man, did you see that?" someone called out.

"Did you see that tank run right over that thing?" another said.

I didn't see any reason for the sergeant to shoot up the truck. It had enough room to turn without causing an accident. I said nothing to the sergeant, but later that night I heard him tell Sergeant Lund, who was asking questions, "What if the truck was cutting us off?" From what I could see, the truck hadn't been shot because it posed a danger to us. It had been shot merely because it had annoyed my sergeant. The truck could have been stopped, or even confiscated. But it was quicker and less trouble all around simply to shoot until it exploded, and blow its driver and passengers—if there were any—to bits. Only six weeks had passed since my arrival in Iraq, but I could already see that, for American soldiers at war, it had become too easy to shoot and too easy to kill. We couldn't catch or see the real insurgents, let alone take a clear shot at them, so civilians would have to do.

In two short weeks in Fallujah, I had already heard gunfire from another division bring down twelve civilians, and I had witnessed my own platoon members killing at least two others. I had seen more blood and death than I cared for, and I felt that we were wrong to be dishing out such violence against civilians. Still, I thought that our military presence was justified in Iraq. I believed we were there to eradicate terrorism, but that the villains had simply not yet shown their faces. Sooner or later, I thought, we would catch them. In the meantime, my job was to follow orders: stand guard, raid houses, and stir shit. I did what I was told and kept my mouth shut.

4

Return to Ramadi

DURING MY FIRST TOUR OF DUTY IN RAMADI, I HAD NO way of knowing that it would be my quietest time in Iraq. Camped so close to the Euphrates River, my squad mates and I stripped down to our underwear one hot afternoon and jumped in the water. We felt carefree for a while and in no real danger, with our weapons set aside, so we shouted and laughed and dunked one another under the water until we saw some small objects floating past us. They were dull green and cube-shaped, each side about six inches long. Unexploded mines. I had learned all about them in military training. If any one of them had blown up, the Euphrates River would have become our

instant grave. We swam to the shore, climbed out on the
bank, got back in our gear, and never again jumped into
the Euphrates.

About a month later, when we returned to the city after
spending two weeks in Fallujah, Ramadi had changed for
the worse. It was no longer a quiet place. It had become
the war zone I had first anticipated when arriving in Iraq,
with one exception—the enemy was never visible.

Almost every night I could hear the mortars being
lobbed toward the former Iraqi military compound that
my 43rd Combat Engineer Company had moved into for
lodgings. The most frightening thing about being mor-
tared was watching the flying bombs become a little more
accurate each time. A mortar comes in different sizes, and
some of them flying toward us were the size of a football,
with little wings on them. I thought of them as long
bombs, lobbed by Iraqi quarterbacks who walked just a
little closer to us each time they let one go. Clearly, the
Iraqi fighters had people stationed near us to indicate how
close the mortars were coming to their targets—us. The
second round would come a little closer, and the third
round even closer, and this we described as the Iraqis
"walking the mortars in on us." Wherever they were—and
we could never see them—they were moving their launchers a little closer.

Initially, the mortars were terrifying. Sometimes I
could make out a faint whir as they sailed through the

air. We called it a "splash" when the mortar exploded, and the kill zone had a radius of some thirty yards. The small, falling bombs kept us jittery and got on our nerves. None of them was big enough to blow up a building. But any one of them, if it landed close enough, could kill us in a second.

Eventually, I learned to sleep through at least some mortar attacks, but not everybody was so lucky. Sergeant Fadinetz, for example, a divorced, thickset man in his mid-thirties who had been in the military for years and had served overseas in South Korea, tried to talk a good game during the day. Sometimes he would lift up his chin and say, "Key, I never want to see you or any of the other sons of bitches in this company once we get out of this war and go home. Once I'm a civilian, as far as I'm concerned, you guys are history. Don't come looking for me, because I won't want to see you." But Fadinetz wasn't as tough as he sounded. He rode with me on top of our armored personnel carrier, told me that he was from Rochester and hoped to go to college one day in Colorado, and I sensed that it took a certain effort for him not to complain about the madness of our assignments in Iraq. You get to know the guys you go to war with, and Fadinetz's fears would come out at night, when the mortars landed and he woke up screaming. I could only imagine the way the sounds of war must have twisted his dreams into nightmares, and I felt for the man as I watched him wake up in terror beside me. Honestly, I didn't know what was worse for him: the nightmares or waking to the sounds of explosions just a little more than a kill zone away.

For many of us in the platoon, adrenaline jolted through our systems like an electric shock and woke us completely—even if we had been sound asleep and had had only an hour of shut-eye in the past day.

It was a strange way to fight a war. We never saw the people who shot at us, never spotted the mortar launchers, and never located the people who used rockets to propel grenades at us. Because our enemy remained invisible, our fears and frustrations mounted, but we could always take those frustrations out on the civilians.

The duty that frightened me the most, in Iraq, was going out with my platoon on foot patrols. We frequently patrolled the streets of Ramadi, trying to engage the enemy, hoping to lure somebody into a firefight. Fortunately for us, the most common thing that happened on our foot patrols was also the worst: once in a while, a man or a child would throw a rock at us. Still, I felt completely vulnerable in those moments. In the thick crowds of people, sometimes I would catch sight of a grenade riding on the tip of a weapon perched on an Iraqi's shoulder. At any moment, I feared, someone would lob a grenade at us or take a clean shot from a rooftop while we were making our way through the crowded markets. Now that we were back for our second tour of duty in the city, few people were smiling at us, and a number made no effort to mask their hatred of us. One day, when a butcher in the market caught me looking at him, he raised his knife and held the sharp edge close to his own throat as I walked by. I swept the rooftops with my eyes, keeping my weapon ready in case I pinpointed a sniper.

Our foot patrols often went on for hours and took place in sweltering heat. Some days in July, I would estimate that the temperature exceeded 120 degrees Fahrenheit. The breeze provided no relief at all; it felt like a gust from a blow-dryer smacking me in the face. Between the uniform, backpack, and M-249, I carried one hundred extra pounds with each step; I would finish the patrols soaked in sweat. Some of the men struggled gravely in the heat. Specialist Sykora became so dehydrated during one long foot patrol that he began to rock back and forth on his heels, like a boxer caught on the chin, and then he crumpled to the ground. We surrounded him to keep him safe and radioed for backup. A Humvee rolled up within minutes. We carried him out to it. He recovered quickly after a medic hooked him up to an intravenous unit.

One day, my platoon mates and I were walking single file through a crowded Ramadi market. Thousands of people were milling about, and I could not stop thinking about the warnings I had been issued by my superiors: the Iraqis were Muslims, and Muslims were terrorists, and I was therefore at risk of attack at any moment. The fruit and the meat stalls were close on either side, and with all of the marketgoers it was hard to stay in contact with the soldier walking in front of me. Suddenly, an Iraqi man cut in front of me, separating me from the soldier ahead of me in our single file. I feared he would try to plunge a knife into me, so I slugged him in the face, pushed by as he stumbled, and ran forward to join my comrades.

It was always with relief that I made it back to the compound at the end of the day. During our second tour of duty in Ramadi, we no longer camped in Saddam Hussein's bombed-out palace. This time, my entire 43rd Combat Engineer Company took over a former Iraqi military compound consisting of several one-story buildings. The compound was located close to the Euphrates River, in central Ramadi. Like most buildings we occupied in Iraqi, it had been bombed earlier by our own forces.

When we moved into the compound, we discovered an Iraqi family of thirteen people—a man with three wives and nine children—inhabiting the facility. I assumed that their own home had been destroyed by American bombs. They had been squatting in there with their clothes, pots and pans, blankets, and all their other possessions. The husband reacted wildly when we commandeered his home. Clearly, he was about to lose the little security that his family had. He shouted at Sayeed, our interpreter, who relayed the message to Captain Conde, who led our company. At the time, I happened to be standing about ten feet away with my squad leader,

Sergeant Padilla. So I was close enough to hear Conde laugh and tell the man, "You've got two hours to get out of here." The man had no choice but to pack up his things and leave with his family.

On other occasions, distraught Iraqis came to us at the compound. While I stood guard, a man entered with his wife and daughter and complained that his daughter had just been raped. I was not able to tell if they were complaining that Americans or Iraqis had committed the crime. I radioed my commander for instructions and was told to send the man off because we couldn't get involved in people's domestic affairs. Another time, a man complained that one of our illumination rounds had crashed into his home and burned his bed. I thought my superiors would send him packing but he was given a small amount of American cash—about $50—and I heard talk among my platoon mates that some officers had a small fund to soothe Iraqis with minor grievances.

As we resumed our regular duties in Ramadi— patrolling streets, checking traffic, guarding buildings, and raiding homes—we began to receive nightly reports from our commanders. When my six squad mates were gathered together at night, our leader—Padilla—would usually read us official army notices. They often contained news items about American soldiers who had been recently killed in Iraq. The notices were like haunting bedtime stories that made all of us more nervous as mortars fell and rocket-propelled grenades exploded closer and closer to us. Just two months earlier, President Bush had flown to the aircraft carrier USS *Abraham Lincoln,* off the coast of San Diego, to give his "mission accomplished" speech. In Iraq, we had heard about the president's speech. "In the battle of Iraq, the United States and our allies have prevailed," the president said. As I listened to the sound of gunfire and explosions, I wished it were true.

Not long into our second tour of duty in Ramadi, I was working at a traffic control point, pulling over vehicles. The standard practice was to order everybody out of the car and to have the driver open the hood and the trunk. A black, four-door Mercedes-Benz pulled up carrying a driver and three male adult passengers. Glancing inside the car, I spotted four grenades tucked between the two front seats.

The driver was a young man, and he didn't say or do anything to provoke me. However, the mere presence of those grenades set me off. I hauled him from the car and began kicking and punching him. An older man in the car began screaming at me in Arabic. I could not understand a word he said, and he would not shut up, so I beat him badly too. By the time I finished with them, both men were bleeding profusely. With the help of my squad mates, I zipcuffed the men, threw one of them in the trunk, and stuffed the other three in the backseat.

Sergeant Fadinetz got into the passenger seat, I jumped into the front, and we drove ten minutes through Ramadi to the police station, where we turned over the men for arrest. I have no idea what became of them, but I do know what happened to their car: I stole it for the use of my squad. We had no keys, so I hot-wired it and attached a switch to make it easy for my squad mates to start. We kept the Mercedes and used it on our house raids, preferring to arrive in an unmarked vehicle to disguise our approach.

When I beat up the two men, I justified it to myself on the grounds that they had grenades in the car. But the truth was that, strange as it may seem to someone outside the war, grenades were everyday items in Iraq, just like the rifles we routinely left behind on our house raids. Although we always confiscated grenades, I had no good reason to attack the men. My own moral judgment was disintegrating under the pressure of being a soldier, feeling vulnerable, and having no clear enemy to kill in Iraq. We were encouraged to beat up on the enemy; given the absence of any clearly understood enemy, we picked our fights with civilians who were powerless to resist. We knew that we would not have to account for our actions. Because we were fearful, sleep-deprived, and jacked up on caffeine, adrenaline, and testosterone, and because our officers constantly reminded us that all Iraqis were our enemies, civilians included, it was tempting to steal, no big deal to punch, and easy to kill. We were Americans in Iraq and we could do anything we wanted to do.

At this time, I was stealing money, knives, and sunglasses from cars and houses. Once I found 1.5 million dinars in an Iraqi truck that I had been assigned to drive to a hospital, and I took that money too. I was not sure how much it was worth, but I imagined about $500. It paid for my cigarettes and Coca-Cola for a while. But one day at a traffic checkpoint, when a man with a large family complained about having no job and no other relatives who could help, I tossed the rest of the money in his backseat and sent him on his way.

Another time, I made a man at a traffic control point remove his artificial leg. Inside it, I found $10,000 in American hundred-dollar bills. I know it was $10,000 because I counted every bill. If my superiors had not been present, I would have considered stuffing it in my pockets and sending it home. But I was flanked by my superior, Sergeant Gurillo, and I gave the money to him when I finished counting it. He handed it to his superior, Captain Bower. I have no idea what happened to the money, but the man with the false leg was carrying on angrily in Arabic and I doubt that he ever got it back.

I am not proud of the things I did in Iraq. However, I will say that before my company left Ramadi, near the end of July, I stopped beating civilians and stopped stealing from them, and I did it no more for the rest of my time in the country. As my conscience began to catch up with me, I witnessed American soldiers and officers losing control of themselves more and more often.

Not long after I beat up the men with the grenades, I found myself yet again at a traffic control point. This time it was late in the evening and we had decided to stop all vehicles that were out past our nighttime curfew of ten p.m. For an hour or two, we stopped about forty taxis and forced the drivers to get out of their vehicles. To their distress, we told them that we were detaining them for breaking the curfew. While some laughed defiantly and others swore, we assembled all the drivers and herded them in small groups into the back of a five-ton truck. A couple of my platoon mates then drove them down to the Ramadi police station, where they were arrested. My superiors instructed me to remain behind and hot-wire the taxis so that the rest of my platoon mates could race them to the police station. A captain of our 43rd Combat Engineer Company (I can't recall for sure which captain it was, as two different captains served during different parts of the month of July) jumped in a taxi and raced with us. For an hour or two that night, my platoon mates had the time of their lives. They bumped and banged the vehicles on their way through the city, but nobody cared. Nobody, that is, in a position to do something about it. I got into the last taxi and took my turn, cranking it up to over sixty miles an hour as I raced through the streets of Ramadi.

We found various other ways to amuse ourselves during quiet moments at the compound. Once again, I earned a few brownie points by hooking up air-conditioning units to the Iraqi power lines. We were supposed to sleep on cots on the main floor, but even with the air conditioners only a small part of the compound was cool enough to sleep in. I often went up to the roof to try to catch some of the evening breeze. Using cinder blocks and an iron bar, I also started weight lifting. Other times, we would hook up portable DVD players to our APC, huddle close together, and watch bootleg movies from our stash, such as *The Hulk* and *House of 1,000 Corpses.*

In my downtime, I chain-smoked, swapped cigarettes with my buddy Private Ricky Connor—a twenty-three-year-old single man from Amarillo, Texas—and teased him mercilessly about how the Oklahoma University Sooners football team spanked his Texas Longhorns team 73–21 while we were at war. We were not allowed to have satellite telephones but some platoon mates kept them anyway, and one of them was able to tell us football scores twenty-four hours after the games had ended. Connor was a patriotic American who believed and seemed to keep on believing that America was doing the right thing in Iraq. Despite my own doubts about the big picture, I liked hanging out with him to talk about Oklahoma and Texas.

We needed our relaxing moments to hang on to our sanity in an increasingly punishing environment. We rarely slept for more than two hours at a time, and frequently we stood guard and conducted other duties for more than twenty-four hours consecutively. At least once a week, officers told us that we were in grave danger of attack. In Fallujah, for example, the soldiers in my company were made to wait in armored vehicles outside a walled compound of old, bombed-out Iraqi military buildings. We were told that ten thousand Iranian supporters of Saddam

Hussein had congregated inside the compound. They were planning to riot, we were told, and we had to be ready for battle. It seemed like a ridiculous story, but I had no choice but to join my fellow soldiers in surrounding the building. We stood outside it for hours while aircraft screamed overhead, Apache helicopters hovered, and Abrams tanks rolled into position. Finally, after hours of waiting and repeated warnings that we were in danger of a riot, the doors were opened. About one hundred unarmed women were let out. There had been no rioters, no weapons, no Hussein sympathizers who had appeared miraculously from Iran, and no threat to our safety.

I believe that the repeated warnings of danger were meant to keep us off guard, and to keep us frightened enough to do exactly what we were told. But what I witnessed was that after a month or two in Iraq, the other soldiers and I could not help but take the warnings less and less seriously, as if they were coming from the boy who cried wolf.

Still, some Iraqis were certainly trying to kill us. We couldn't see them but they were there. A man named Sergeant Taylor, who worked with another platoon in my company, was driving across Ramadi in a Humvee when a bomb blew up under the vehicle. My squad mates and I had been guarding a bank at the time, and we were ordered to race across Ramadi in our APC to help out. We found Sergeant Taylor—who was overdue to return home to the States—with an eye hanging out of his face and shrapnel wounds across his body. He was evacuated for medical care, and as far as I know he lived. The next night, we were told to raid houses in the neighborhood in retaliation for the attack on the Humvee. One of my sergeants said, "Tonight it's retaliation time against the city of Ramadi."

We carried on with our house raids, ransacking houses and detaining every man we could find.

A short time later Sergeant Padilla woke me up at about one a.m. to tell me to climb out of my sleeping bag and get ready for action. Our platoon was designated a Quick Reaction Force, and our orders were to rush to help out American soldiers from the 124th Infantry Division who were said to be caught in a firefight with hundreds of Iraqis. I did not believe the story. I had yet to see one Iraqi militant rioting and shooting, so it seemed unlikely to me that I would now find hundreds doing so.

My six squad mates and I jumped in our APC, and I took my usual position on the top left of the vehicle, training my machine gun on rooftops as we drove in formation with the other two APCs in our platoon.

I rode up top with Fadinetz and Padilla. Down below, Mason drove the APC while Jones, Sykora, and Lewis sat inside with him. Sergeant Jones shouted that we were on our way to face hundreds of rioting Iraqis in an alley. Fadinetz and I shared a private laugh over this, because we both felt it was highly unlikely. We rode slowly for about ten minutes. We made two turns in our APC and, while traveling at just a few miles an hour, moved toward the banks of the Euphrates River along a small road that we called "the red route." I could make out the sounds of a firefight.

It was about two a.m., but I could see very well because there were streetlights on our road and because of the American illumination rounds that kept the sky lit up all night.

Suddenly, I looked over to my left and saw the bodies of four decapitated Iraqis in their bloodied white robes, lying a few feet from a bullet-ridden pickup truck to the side of the road. Because I sat on the top left of the vehicle, and because the bodies were on the left-hand side of the road, I had them in clear view. I assumed that someone had used a massive amount of gunfire to behead them.

"Shit," I said.

A few seconds later, our slow-moving APC came to a stop. Among the three APCs in our convoy, I was the only soldier immediately ordered down to the ground. As I slid down into the APC and then out the hatch, Sergeant Jones told me to look for brass casings, which would be signs that Iraqi fighters with AK-47s had been shooting at American soldiers in the area.

I saw no sign of brass casings, but I did see an American soldier shouting at the top of his lungs while two other soldiers stood quietly next to him.

"We fucking lost it, we just fucking lost it," the soldier was shouting. He was in a state of complete distress, but the soldiers next to him were not reacting. The distressed soldier stood about twenty yards from me, and another forty or so yards from the four decapitated bodies.

Two other soldiers were laughing and kicking the heads of the decapitated Iraqis. It was clearly a moment of amusement for them. This was their twisted game of soccer.

I froze at the sight of it, and for a moment could not believe my eyes. But I saw what I saw, and was so revolted and horrified that I defied Sergeant Jones's orders and climbed right back into the APC.

"I'm not having anything to do with that," I said. I wondered who the soldiers could possibly be, what their rank was, and who their commanding officer was, but I had not been able to see any of the details in the brief time I was on the ground.

Jones looked at me like I was crazy for defying him, but I was not sure if he had seen what I had seen. I doubted it, because he was stuck down inside the APC and it was facing in the opposite direction of the heads that the soldiers had been kicking.

On the radio, Lieutenant Joyce—who was in one of the other APCs—asked Sergeant Padilla why I had gotten back in my vehicle, but I was too shocked to offer an answer. I just climbed back to my spot on top of the APC and—like my fellow soldiers—faced in the opposite direction of the bodies and the heads. We were still supposedly protecting the American soldiers on the ground from attack. We remained in that one spot for another thirty or forty minutes, holding our position, facing down an alley, preparing for the promised onslaught of rioting Iraqis. They never came. As far as I could see, the only armed men in the area were American soldiers from the 124th Infantry

Division and from my own 43rd Combat Engineer Company. Finally, we spun around 180 degrees to return to the compound. As we began to roll I could see the four decapitated bodies again as well as the shot-up truck, but I could no longer see the heads.

Our APC moved slowly forward, then suddenly swerved so sharply that I nearly lost my balance. I had no idea why Mason, who was driving, had made us swerve like that.

Later, I asked Sykora if he had seen what I had seen. He said nothing at all but just looked through me with the thousand-mile stare, a sort of trance that made him appear to be looking off into space.

The compound, when we returned to it, seemed even less safe to me than it had before. Like most of the other military buildings and palaces, it had been bombed before we'd gotten there. I couldn't sleep in it or walk through it without having bits of concrete and dust fall on my head. I stood guard duty for a few hours, and as I was finishing I went to our urinals to relieve myself. There, I found myself standing beside Mason, our APC driver, who was about to begin guard duty.

"Hey, man, you nearly made me fall off the APC," I said. "Why the hell did you swerve like that?"

"I was trying to run over one of the heads," he said.

"You've gone right fucking nuts," I told him.

Mason gave me a furious look, and our conversation went no further.

I was revolted that Mason had tried to join in on the mutilation of the heads. The killing of the four Iraqis, the games American soldiers played with their heads, the silence of my own military commanders when we came upon the scene, and Mason's attempt to join in on the act all combined to snap the last threads of belief I had in my country and what it was doing at war. I had always seen my fellow Americans as upholders of justice in the world, but now I had come face to face with the indecency of our actions in Iraq.

Later that morning, I asked Sergeant Skillings about the soldiers who had been out with us at the Euphrates, and he confirmed that they belonged to the Florida National Guard, part of the 124th Infantry Division. I hoped that someone would write a report about the events of the night, and I naively asked Sergeant Padilla if I could see it. He told me that it was none of my damn business and that I should leave it alone. I had expected such an answer but had not been able to prevent myself from asking the question in the first place. It was too horrendous an act to be left unreported, yet Padilla's response led me to suspect that my commanding officers would not write a single word about the incident.

I didn't raise the matter again, but the event changed the way I thought about my army in this war.

I didn't know much about the Geneva Conventions, but I knew one thing: what I had witnessed was wrong. We were soldiers of the U.S. Army. In Iraq, we were supposed to be stomping out terrorism, bringing democracy, and acting as a force for good in the world. Instead we had become monsters in a residential neighborhood. Civilians in houses just fifty yards away could easily have been watching as soldiers in the American army had not only shot dead four civilians but used an outrageous amount of gunfire to cut off their heads. I didn't have to be a lawyer to know that armies at war were not supposed to rape, plunder, loot, or pillage. They were not supposed to harm civilians or mutilate the bodies of the dead. I was so troubled that I could not speak about the incident.

My grandparents were far from perfect people, but I had learned one or two fundamental lessons growing up on their farm. It was wrong to attack defenseless people. And if you did get into a fight, it would be utterly despicable to start kicking your opponent once he was down. When I was back home in Oklahoma, if somebody had described the situation of the decapitated corpses, I would have had a hard time believing it. I would not have wanted to accept that American soldiers would behave in this way overseas. But I was no longer in Oklahoma and I could not deny what I had seen.

For the rest of my time in Iraq I was not able to forget the scene of the decapitated bodies and the heads being kicked by American soldiers. Sometimes, in my dreams, disembodied heads plagued me with accusations. They told me what I was slowly realizing: that the American military had betrayed the values of my country. We had become a force for evil, and I could not escape the fact that I was part of the machine.

5

The Girl at the Hospital

SPECIALIST SYKORA WAS HOOKED ON DEAN KOONTZ novels, "007" and "Splinter Cell" on his Game Boy, and World Wrestling Federation matches. He was originally from Chicago, but his wife and children lived in Ohio. He said his wife would not let him get out of the military because they needed the salary and the health insurance benefits. He hoped to change his life one day and learn how to repair small engines, but he had been stalled in the military for many years and was already thirty-six. In the army world, I wondered if he had become a lifer.

Not long after the four Iraqi civilians were shot and beheaded, Sykora and I decided to get drunk. Even though there were strict rules against drinking while we were at war, we took a chance anyway, trying to drown our anxieties in beer and a bottle of Jordanian whiskey.

We were in shock over the deaths but we were also worked up over Captain Bower, who had recently taken over command of our company. Bower was tall and thin and wore glasses. He had a direct and forceful personality, and I didn't like him. Bower knew that his soldiers had been complaining about the day-to-day dangers, so he addressed the matter head-on in a meeting of our platoon. He poked me in the chest and at the same time began lecturing Sergeant Fadinetz. "You know what, Sergeant?" he said. "Your dangers don't matter to me. If one hundred of you walk out that door, as long as seventy-five percent of you walk back inside I'm a happy man because it's an acceptable fatality rate."

Sykora and I got the message then and there that we were little more than numbers in the eyes of our superiors. We felt that it didn't really matter to our commanders whether we lived or died. Feeling that we were expendable commodities gave Sykora and me all the more to complain about as we sought shelter in an isolated part of the compound—one that nobody was supposed to enter because our own air force had bombed it so thoroughly that nobody knew when the entire structure would fall in—and downed our beer and whiskey.

Food was another source of distraction to us. Two black men in my company refused to eat the military rations and instead used their pocket money to buy lamb sandwiches daily at $2 a pop. I liked those sandwiches too and ate a few of them, smothered in Tabasco and ketchup. They came straight from an Iraqi vendor who cooked large legs of lamb on a rotisserie by the side of the road.

Even as we broke into their houses, patrolled their streets, and stopped their cars, Iraqi vendors kept coming at us. They sold clothing, pipes, and cigarettes. They sold kebabs, Coke, and ice. They sold porn videos. They sold bootleg movies shot with handheld cameras inside movie theaters. Our food was so bad and we were so bored that we kept those vendors in business. I spent about $50 a month on food, drinks, and souvenirs from street vendors. Some of the guys in my platoon spent more.

One man in my company—a bone-thin nineteen-year-old named Private Lewis—had a mom back in Illinois who made the best damn beef jerky in the world. Hot and spicy, it lit a fire at the back of my throat. Whenever Lewis received a care package from home, I got a big wad of beef jerky and stretched it out as long as I could.

However, for most of us, there was no getting around our staple food, the military rations called Meals Ready to Eat, or MREs for short. We were supposed to eat three of them a day. Most soldiers agreed that the MREs were among the grossest foods known to man. In its almost indestructible package, the dried food was said to last up to ten years. For a soldier at war, the food was mostly about convenience: an MRE actually heats itself up. You stick a package inside a package, add a bit of water, and the stuff starts bubbling and boiling on its own. You have a hot meal in a minute or two—but that didn't

mean we thought they were edible. I made up my own nick-
names: *Beef Screw* (beef stew), *Please Relieve Me* (cheese
tortellini), *Stork Piss* (pork rib), and *Gun Powder* (clam
chowder). I could stomach just one of the MREs, and I
let my squad mates know that no man's life was safe if he
took it. The beef enchilada was mine and mine only.
When I drowned it in Tabasco sauce, the enchilada reminded me vaguely of Mexican food in Oklahoma. Apart
from bringing back the taste of home, the beef enchilada
had one other advantage: it wasn't ruined by the presence
of vegetables. I'm not your vegetable sort of guy. As far as
I'm concerned, vegetables are what food eats.

When my squad mates and I traveled in our armored personnel carrier to do guard duty at the Ramadi
children's hospital, we took our MREs along with us.
Because our duties usually lasted for twenty-four hours,
we kept a stash of MREs in the APC parked outside the
hospital. While changing posts at the hospital every four
or so hours, I was free to grab an MRE and a bottle of
water.

Guard duty at the hospital was mentally draining.
There was always the threat of danger, so we were required to have our weapons locked and ready to fire. However, nothing ever seemed to happen, which made the days
go by slowly. When the sun beat down on us it was hard
to find an inch of shade.

Sometimes, while standing guard on the roof, I
would chat with a middle-aged doctor named Muhammad
who came outside on his breaks to smoke cigarettes and

look out over the city. He spoke English well, asked about my family, and told me that he had seventeen children. One day, while he fiddled with the stethoscope around his neck, he said that two of his sons had been hanged in Ramadi by Saddam Hussein's men. He didn't care for Saddam Hussein, he said, but he didn't like having Americans in the city either.

"Where are you from?" he asked.

I told him a little about life in Oklahoma. Like many Iraqis, he seemed stunned to be told that I had grown up poor. But he was heartened to hear that I had a wife and three sons.

"So when do you think the U.S. troops will pull out?" he asked.

"I have no idea," I said, "but I've got a feeling we're going to be here for a long, long time."

He grimaced.

"I've got to tell you," I added, "I'm looking forward to getting out of here just as much as you would like to see me gone."

He laughed at that. I asked what he had been doing before the war began, and he mentioned that he had taught medicine at universities in Ramadi and Baghdad. I had heard talk about how difficult it was for Iraqi hospitals to get medical supplies after the first Gulf War and was going to ask him about that, but an angry voice crackled on my walkie-talkie. It was one of my superiors.

"Key! Get away from that man and stop fraternizing with the enemy."

Muhammad returned to the roof at other times, however, which gave us more opportunities to chat. He liked his cigarettes, and we had that in common.

"What do you do in Oklahoma?"

"Whatever jobs I can find," I said. "Painting, delivering pizza, but welding is what I really want to do."

"My country could use a few welders," he said.

"Over here, this is just a job for me, and it's not making any sense to me either," I said.

"A job?" he repeated with a puzzled look. "You're different from most of the Americans here."

The next time we met outside the hospital, Muhammad gave me a small edition of the Qur'an. It was in Arabic, but I was touched by the gift. Before any of my superiors could notice, I slid the book quickly into my trouser pocket.

"I hope this will help you," he said, "and that you will return home safely to the ones who love you."

I thought of Muhammad, and of how difficult his job must be, each time I walked through the hospital corridors and upstairs to the roof. The trips were depressing. I shuddered at the thought of needing treatment in such a filthy place. Needles were scattered all over the floors and by toilets, and I spotted blood and fetuses. I imagined that the tiny, half-formed bodies had come from miscarriages, and I stopped to think about how hard the war had to be on the women of Iraq. Given that the hospital lacked the equipment to properly dispose of needles and fetuses, it gave me the shivers to imagine the conditions in which the living were treated. I wondered to what degree our occupation of the country had caused all these problems in the hospital, and admired Muhammad and the other doctors and nurses for trying to save the lives of diseased and injured children.

Standing guard for twenty-four hours in a row probably killed more brain cells than alcohol. It was mind-numbing. I smoked cigarettes, chewed Copenhagen dip, knocked back shots of Tabasco sauce, bought Coca-Cola from street vendors, wondered how Brandi and our boys were doing on the base in Colorado and whether the arm Adam had broken just before I flew to Iraq had healed, and I welcomed any distractions to stay awake. One such distraction that I learned to anticipate and enjoy came in the form of daily visits from a young Iraqi girl who lived with her family in a house across the street from the hospital.

I wish I knew the girl's name, but she spoke almost no English and I knew no Arabic. She was about seven years old. She had dark eyes, shoulder-length brown hair, and—even for a young child—seemed impossibly skinny. She usually wore her school uniform—a white shirt with a blue skirt and a pair of sandals. Every time I was stationed outside the hospital, the girl would run up to the fence that ran between us and call out the only English words she knew: "Mister, food." Over and over she would say that, and I can still recall her high-pitched, breathless enthusiasm. She seemed fearless, full of energy, and not the least bit frightened by my M-249. She acted as if she didn't even know that she lived in a war zone, and she ran to the fence the same way my own children might have approached a sandbox, piping out, "Mister, food."

During my first tour of duty in Ramadi in May, and in my second time there in late June and July, I stood guard at that hospital on at least thirty occasions. She ran up to the fence every single time I was posted on duty there. I sat just inches away, on a big rock, but I would stand to greet her when she came up to me. I wondered who had taught her to say these two English words. Perhaps it was her mother, who often stood at the door of their ramshackle house, waiting for the girl to bring food for the family.

The first time she ran up to me I tried to ignore her. We were under orders not to speak to Iraqi civilians at all, unless authorized to do so by one of our officers. I knew that it would be better for me to have nothing to do with her, and it didn't seem like a good thing for a seven-year-old child to be anywhere near American soldiers standing with assault rifles locked and ready at all times.

"Mister! Food!"

"Go away," I said.

"Mister, food."

I waved my hand to tell her to go away because she clearly wasn't getting my words.

She kept at me, and I started mumbling at her. "Come on, little sister, you've really got to get out of here."

She stood motionless, kept smiling, and would not leave. Finally, I reached over the four-foot-high, chain-link fence and handed her my MRE. It was a beef enchilada with Tabasco sauce, a packet of cheese, a few crackers, two pieces of gum, a bag of Skittles, a pouch of powder to make an orange drink, and a pack of matches. The whole thing came in a thick, tightly sealed plastic bag about a foot long, six inches deep, and three inches wide. It weighed less than a pound. She took it, turned, and ran with it back to her house. I don't know how her family got into that thing. The instructions in small print on the bag were only in English. I don't know if her family members figured out that you had to break open one pouch, pour in water, and let it boil for a minute or so before you ate it. I had no idea what a poor Iraqi family would make of food that was made to feed men on the moon. Perhaps it would be so bad that she would never come back.

But three days later, when I returned for another day of guard duty at the hospital, there she was, racing out of her house, across the small street, and up to the fence where I stood.

"Mister! Food."

Her face and her feet were dirty. It occurred to me that it must be extremely hard to keep a child clean in a country with a destroyed infrastructure and a ruptured water supply.

I tried once more to wave her off, but she would have nothing of it. She stood her ground until I tossed her an MRE. This time, I had a different flavor stashed in my pants cargo pocket. Country Captain Chicken, along with a package of peanut butter, a container of grape jam, a slice of bread in vacuum-sealed plastic, a piece of poppy seed lemon cake, peppermint gum, and the drink powder. I handed it over. She smiled, took it, and ran off with it. When she got to her front door, though, I saw her mother slap her and send her right back out to me.

"Mister. More food." Ah. A third word. She resisted my warnings to get clear of danger and stayed until I managed to fetch another MRE. I radioed one of my buddies in the squad to get an MRE from the APC and bring it to me. This time it was beef teriyaki.

She did not get slapped again when she returned with the second package, and I wondered if her family had ever seen peanut butter and jam, or what they thought of Country Captain Chicken. It struck me that they had a pretty dismal picture of American life: M-249s and the world's fastest yet least edible food.

As my guarding duties at the hospital continued, I began to carry a small stash of MREs with me so that I could give her two at a time.

The girl always ran home with them. She never walked. It seemed like running was the only speed she knew. It didn't matter if it was 125 degrees in the afternoon sun. When the girl moved, she ran. It made me happy to see her flying across the street on those light brown legs.

I wondered what sort of life she would have when the war ended. Would she continue in school? Would she end up becoming a doctor or a teacher?

Her visits were the best part of my days at the hospital, and she was the only person in Iraq—officer, civilian, or fellow soldier—whose smile I enjoyed. From my earliest childhood, I have distrusted the smiles of adults because I always wonder what they know that I don't. The smile of this child in Ramadi brought me to thoughts of my own wife and children. I wished that Brandi could see this girl and discover what I was coming to know: it was not true that all Muslims were terrorists, children included. The truth was that this little girl was the same as any child growing up in Oklahoma, Colorado, or any other part of the world: all she needed was a little food, a little schooling, a clean supply of water, and some loving adults to take care of her. She was no terrorist. She was nothing but a child, and everything about her—waving arms, uncombed hair, and torn sandals—reminded me that she and her family had the same needs as I did. All they wanted was food, water, shelter, safety, school, and work—who didn't?

I wasn't the only soldier in our squad who gave rations to the girl. Sykora did it too, and we spoke of her often.

"I saw that girl today while I was out front of the hospital," Sykora would say.

"Give her anything this time?" I'd ask.

"Damn right," he would say. "Beef stew and a bottle of water."

As the visits continued, I noticed little things about her. She seemed to have a slight limp when she ran. Each time she came, as soon as I tossed her one or two MREs, I would say, "Hey there, little sister. You really have to get going. Go. Don't stay here. Go home now."

I didn't want her to stay long because every time Lieutenant Joyce saw me handing her food he scolded me for fraternizing with the enemy. When she stood too long at the fence, I would toss candies—Werther's and Starburst, for example—far enough away to get her to move to a safer spot.

As for the MREs, I gave her a bit of everything we had, including chicken salsa and beef steak. It all tasted like dog food to me, but it could keep you alive in a pinch, and this little girl and her family needed them more than I did. When she got the food she would smile, give me a little bow, then turn and run back home.

After I had gone to Fallujah and then returned to Ramadi, the girl noticed me again perched on a rock at the corner of the fence, and she began running to me daily again, asking for food. I would also give her bottles of water.

One day she brought me a piece of bread. When it passed over the fence, from her hand to mine, I could feel that it was still warm.

"Fresh baked?" I said.

She smiled and waited for me to eat it.

It was a flat bread, and delicious, and she would not move until I had eaten the whole thing.

"Thank you," I said.

The next day she brought me a glass of water.

I knew it was probably straight out of the Euphrates River, but I wanted to please her so I drank it straight-away. It was nastier than hell, but I was happy to do that for her.

I was away on house raids for a few days after that, and I found myself looking forward to guard duty at the hospital so that I could see the little girl again.

The next week, I was back at my post in front of the hospital. I saw the girl run out of her house, across the street, and toward the fence that stood between us. I reached for an MRE, looked up to see her about ten feet away, heard the sound of semiautomatic gunfire, and saw her head blow up like a mushroom.

Her death was so abrupt and such a shock that I couldn't believe what I had seen. I looked around immediately after she was killed. There were no armed Iraqis within sight, and I had not heard any of the steady drilling sound made by the Iraqi AK-47s. The only thing I had heard was the distinctive sound of an M-16, which doesn't give off a loud, sustained burst of gunfire. It sounds much weaker than the AK-47 and shoots just a few bullets at a time. *Pop pop pop.* Break. *Pop pop pop.* Break.

I looked in every direction. The only armed people in the area were my squad mates, posted at various points around and on top of the hospital. My own people were the only ones with guns in the area, and it was the sound of my own people's guns that I had heard blazing before the little sister was stopped in her tracks.

I saw her mother fly out the door and run across the street. She and someone else in the family bent over the body. I could feel them all staring at me, and I could say nothing to them and do nothing other than hang my head in shame while the family took the child away.

Even today I can't help thinking that it was one of my own guys who did it. And I can't help feeling that I was responsible for her death. If I hadn't been feeding her, and allowing her to believe that it was safe to come by daily to say "Mister, food" and to scoop up the MREs that I'd give her, little sister might be alive today. She would be about ten years old now, around the same age as my eldest son, Zackary.

Her death haunts me to this day. I am trying to learn to live with it.

6

al-Habbaniyah

NEAR THE BEGINNING OF AUGUST 2003, THE 43RD COM-
bat Engineer Company left Ramadi and moved about ten
miles east to al-Habbaniyah. It was a small, dusty town of
no more than ten thousand people, set on the banks of the
Euphrates River. Close to al-Habbaniyah, there was a vil-
lage named Khaldia. In this book, when I write about
events in al-Habbaniyah, I mean the area including it and
Khaldia. We spent the next six weeks there raiding houses
and patrolling streets and guarding munitions depots as
well as our own compound.

The Bible says that the Euphrates River was one of
four flowing out of the Garden of Eden. I wish we had
found peace by the calm waters bordering the town, but by

this time tensions in Iraq had escalated so much that we were under regular attack from fighters we could never see.

As a group of soldiers, if we stopped in any one place and stayed more than twenty minutes, mortars and rocket-propelled grenades would start raining on us. When I found myself alive at the end of a dangerous day, I sometimes imagined that, just like a cat, I had been granted nine lives. Even so, they were being used up quickly. Around this time, my squad mates and I were on foot patrol on the streets of al-Habbaniyah when rocket-propelled grenades started falling on us. I could hear them whizzing through the air. They were about half the size of a football but something of a blur as they flew nearby just above my head. I would have been injured if any of them had blown up within thirty yards of me, and dead if it happened within ten yards. I dashed for the cover of a concrete wall. Before I could make it, a grenade flew by me and hit the ground just inches away. I expected to be shredded by red-hot shrapnel but the grenade bounced, rolled, and failed to explode. I kept running and took shelter behind the wall. There was no wake-up call more brutal than a close encounter with a grenade. It was nastier than ten shots of Tabasco or five cups of coffee. As my pounding heart slowed I thought that sooner or later my time would come.

Being attacked so often by invisible enemies made all of us in the squad more and more anxious. We didn't like being shot at, didn't like not having anybody to shoot back at, and we wondered if we would ever get home alive.

I didn't get to call Brandi often. About five weeks went by in Iraq before I could make my first call home, and usually three more weeks would pass before I'd have another chance to call. Sometimes I would stand for hours in line, waiting for my turn on a military telephone. Some days, I would get my two minutes on the line and get through to my wife. Other times, before I could make it to the front of the line, I would have to report back to duty. I loved hearing from Brandi, and reassuring her that I was just fine, and I loved hearing her voice and receiving her weekly letters. However, throughout my time in Iraq, those words from Sergeant Jones kept ringing in my ears. "Your wife is gonna start fucking some other guy the moment you're out of the country," he had said. "You wait. You'll see. It happens to them all." That little bastard had known exactly how to upset me, and the seed of distrust embedded itself in my mind. I trusted Brandi and believed that she would stick by me until death parted us. Yet my heart was a different thing, and my heart worried.

Some soldiers lost their lives in Iraq, and others lost their limbs. A few were worried sick about matters at home. One private from Alaska heard that his wife had developed brain cancer. After waiting some time, he was allowed to fly home.

On one occasion, when I was next in line for the phone, I overheard a specialist in my company talking to his wife. There was no privacy whatsoever on the military telephones, and I could even hear her talking back to him. I could hear her saying that she was leaving him, and then I could hear a man bark into the line, "Your little bitch wife is my princess now." And then the line went dead. I signaled to the fellow that I could wait and that it was all right with me if he picked up the telephone and called home again. He dialed the number and got his wife on the line. She told him that he would be getting separation papers in the mail. The soldier broke down and cried just as freely as a child. There was nothing for me to do but put my arm around him and hold him as his body shook.

A soldier named Foster, from Indiana, was thrilled when he got the chance to go home on a short vacation. I wished him the best, but I wasn't optimistic about how things would go because we all knew that he hadn't received a single letter from his wife during our months in Iraq and that his home telephone number had been disconnected. Foster was given two weeks off, but after ten days he was back. I asked him why he had returned early.

"My wife left me, sold everything we had, ran up our credit card, and took off," he said. "I have nothing left, so I might as well be here."

Our morale was dropping, but so was that of Sayeed, the nineteen-year-old Iraqi who traveled with our company. Since our first days in Iraq, he had been insisting to me and to some of the other soldiers that our commanders had promised him that if he kept serving them for $20 a week, running errands and translating to and from Arabic, they would bring him to America and let him live there.

"It's a pack of lies," I told him. "There's no way in hell they're going to take you back with them."

"The captain said it was true, and he knows more than you," Sayeed said.

As time went on in Iraq, Sayeed saw no indications that he would be going to the United States. True, he kept drawing his $20 a week. But he also began getting death threats from Iraqis who saw him as a traitor. As the conditions of war worsened in the country, Sayeed became nervous and agitated. When he had first begun working for the 43rd CEC as an interpreter and errand boy, he had walked freely in the streets of Ramadi. But by the time we had set up in al-Habbaniyah, he would not leave our military compound without us. I wondered if he thought his meager salary and the shaky promise of a new life in America were worth the threats.

Occasionally I hand-washed my underwear and socks and let them dry under the boiling sun, but I never had the chance to wash my sleeping bag. I spread it out in our new lodgings in al-Habbaniyah—as usual, a former military compound that had been blasted with our own bombs. We set up a gate around the compound, a dormitory and meeting quarters. At night, all the soldiers in my platoon bunked together in one room. We each had a cot but they were only a foot apart, and it seemed that some of the men had given up entirely on sleep. Lying still on a cot could open the doors to memories and nightmares, and for some it was easier to escape the night by watching movies on portable screens, playing Game Boys, reading books, or masturbating. I had just as many anxieties as my buddies in Iraq but was lucky not to have any sleeping problems. I could sleep inside a tank and through a mortar attack, so the sound of ten men snoring was nothing to me.

Each American military company was responsible for dealing with the bodies of the civilians it had killed, so one of my first and most unpleasant duties in al-Habbaniyah was to build a shack in which to store dead Iraqis until someone came to claim them. We set the shack near our front gate so that relatives could retrieve their loved ones without entering our compound.

I began to discover that I was becoming almost as much a danger to myself as the Iraqi resistance fighters. Every time I stepped out of our compound gate, I was aware that I might not make it back alive. I frequently thought about shooting myself in the foot so that I could be removed from war and taken back home. Other soldiers talked about doing it too. With all the bullets and grenades in the air, we didn't think it would be such a big deal to take our own little shot. We didn't think of the pain, or of the fact that we would be dealing with that injury for the rest of our lives. All we thought was that a well-placed self-injury was manageable and that it would get us out of harm's way in Iraq. Back home in America, you would have to be pretty far gone to think seriously about shooting yourself. But at war in Iraq, with shrapnel exploding around you every day and notices being read to us almost nightly about our fellow soldiers killed in various parts of the country, and coasting on so little shut-eye that I felt as if I were sleepwalking in my daytime maneuvers, self-injury seemed like a normal thought.

We knew one man who had already done it and another who had spoken openly of suicide. Shortly before coming to al-Habbaniyah, a specialist named Love loaded his M-16 grenade launcher while he was standing on guard duty at our compound. I was changing the oil on our armored personnel carrier at the time, only about fifty yards away, when I heard the thump of the grenade and the soldier screaming. Sergeant Fadinetz, a few other soldiers, and I ran over to Love.

"What happened?" we asked him, but he would not say.

We could see that Love had shot himself in the ankle and we called for help. He was taken away for medical care, and we never saw him again. It was a good thing the grenade had not exploded or he could have been killed.

"Guess he's going home now," I said. Wherever home was, we assumed that Love eventually made it there.

I talked about the incident with the buddies in my squad but none of us judged him, because we admitted we had all thought about doing the same thing.

I heard about a sergeant in my company who raised his nine-millimeter semiautomatic pistol, banged himself on the head with it, and said that he was going to kill himself. He too was sent home.

One day, Captain Bower walked into our sleeping area, told us to gather around our cots, and read us a notice passed down from his superiors. It said that any soldier who shot himself would be patched up in Germany and sent right back into action.

I believed he was serious, and stopped thinking so much of hurting myself, but I often considered another strategy and tried it a few times. While we took cover from flying bullets and shrapnel, sometimes I stuck out my arm in harm's way, hoping that an enemy bullet might smash into it. Although I was a good shot with a rifle, I luckily wasn't very good at getting shot, and no bullet or scrap of red-hot metal—shot by an enemy or shot by myself—took me down during the months I served in Iraq. Others in my squad talked about doing this too, and we would sometimes joke about it after a firefight.

"I guess you didn't manage to take one in the arm this time," I would say to one of my buddies.

"No, maybe next time" the answer would come back.

Nevertheless, we resented the fact that we wore flak jackets of inferior quality, dating back to the Vietnam War. We may have thought about injuring ourselves, but that didn't mean we wanted to die.

One day, a colonel came to al-Habbaniyah to give us a pep talk. Just before we assembled to hear him speak, Captain Bower warned us to keep our mouths shut and not to ask any questions. After the pep talk the colonel invited questions. Nobody said a thing. The colonel reassured us that it was okay to tell him whatever was on our minds. Specialist Williams, who was in the second squad of my platoon, asked why the men had not received proper flak jackets. I saw Lieutenant Joyce and Sergeant Padilla giving Williams the evil eye; the colonel brushed him off.

A little later Williams came to speak to me. He looked furious. "They are docking half of my pay for three months just for asking a fucking question," he said.

I estimate that he lost at least $2,000 in salary, but we received the better-quality bulletproof vests—called interceptors—within a matter of days. A number of soldiers thanked Williams for speaking up, but nothing we said could bring back his docked pay.

Most of us in the platoon had one reason or another for resenting our superiors. A sergeant was disciplined because he was caught drinking liquor with us while on guard duty. He was the only one punished, because he was highest ranking, and that didn't sit well with him at all.

Like my buddies, I nursed my own grievances. Chief among them was the duty that fell on my shoulders every second day: to ignite, stir, and burn all the shit in our toilets. Perhaps it helped us all to have some trivial point to be angry about. Maybe the anger motivated us to keep on stumbling from one day to the next.

One day, however, something new replaced shit burning as my pet peeve. I was sitting on my cot when one of Captain Bower's aides came for me.

"The captain wants to see you," he said.

When I walked into the captain's makeshift office, he told me that Brandi had caused a disturbance on the base at Fort Carson. I had no idea what he was talking about.

"You'd better learn to control your wife, Private," he said.

It crossed my mind that I stirred his shit too. I should have kept my stupid mouth shut, but instead I said, "That's kind of hard, Captain, when she's thousands of miles away."

"Well, Private, because of that, you won't be getting any more rank," the captain said.

By that he meant that I would remain a private forever and not reach even the rank of specialist. Nor would my pay increase.

I walked out of his office with one more thing to stew about and, perhaps, one more distraction from falling mortars and grenades.

Busting into and ransacking homes remained one of my most common duties in Iraq. I had done it in Fallujah and in Ramadi and now I found the tasks continuing in al-Habbaniyah. Before my time was up in Iraq, I took part in about two hundred raids. But by the time I had made it to al-Habbaniyah I had lost all belief that we had good reason for the raids. We never found weapons or indications of terrorism. I never found a thing that seemed to justify the terror we inflicted every time we blasted through the front door of a civilian home, broke everything in sight, punched and zipcuffed the men, and sent them away.

I had no choice but to continue with the raids, and I remained the one who set the plastic explosive, blew up the door, and ran inside as the third squad member with my rifle locked and ready. But I had stopped shouting at people by the time I got to al-Habbaniyah, stopped roughing them up, and stopped stealing from them. I had no more heart in the work and believed that it did nothing except intimidate the Iraqis, destroy their few belongings, and inspire them to hate us.

We took part in many raids in al-Habbaniyah, but two stand out in my memory.

For the first of these raids, we were told at three a.m. to get up and go to a home that was suspected of having a cache of weapons. They dropped off our entire platoon of twenty guys near the river, saying that the house was only two hundred yards away. We couldn't find the house and got lost. We struggled for a good hour in a rice paddy by the river. It was hotter than hell, even before dawn. Along with our regular equipment we lugged pickaxes that we had received recently as a tool to use in our searches. We finally came up to a house. It resembled the photos we'd been given. We punched our location into the GPS and it matched the coordinates we'd been given.

It was a handsome two-story house and quite isolated. Along with my usual squad members—with the exception of Specialist Mason, who had returned home and been replaced by Specialist Barrigan—I ran up to the house. As usual, I put the charge of C-4 explosives on the door and we blew it in.

As we rushed into the house, women were staggering out of their rooms. Three teenage girls screamed when they saw us. Some of my squad mates grabbed them and held them at gunpoint, and the rest of us ran through the house. We found no men at all, just six more women in their twenties and thirties.

The guys in my squad couldn't find a thing—not even any guns—and it seemed that the more incapable they were of locating contraband, the more destructive they became. They smashed dressers, ripped mattresses, broke cabinets, and threw shelves to the floor.

I said, "What the hell are you guys doing? There's not even a single male in this house."

But on they went, until somebody had the bright idea that weapons were likely hidden under the floor. So out came the pickaxes and the guys started busting up the floor, going through the rug, the tiles, and into the concrete.

It was so ludicrous that it was almost funny. Here were my guys trying to break through a concrete floor with pickaxes. If weapons had been stored under the rug, you'd think that the tiles would have given way quickly to a secret hiding spot—not a uniform foundation of concrete running all the way across the floor. But this destruction continued for ten or fifteen minutes. When it became obvious even to the guys busting the concrete floor that there was nothing in the house but a number of angry women, we went back outside.

I found Private First Class Hayes with a woman under an empty carport. He pointed his M-16 at her head but she would not stop screaming.

"What are you doing this for?" she said.

Hayes told her to shut up.

"We have done nothing to you," she went on.

Hayes was starting to lose it, and we weren't even supposed to be talking to this woman. I told her that we were there on orders and that we couldn't speak to her, but on and on and on she bawled at Hayes and me.

"You Americans are disgusting! Who do you think you are, to do this to us?"

Hayes slammed her in the face with the stock of his M-16. She fell facedown into the dirt, bleeding and silent. The woman lay still on the ground. I pushed Hayes away.

"What are you doing, man?" I said to him. "You have a wife and two kids! Don't be hitting her like that."

He looked at me with eyes full of hatred, as if he was ready to kill me for saying those words, but he did not touch the woman again. I found this incident with Hayes particularly disturbing because during other times I had seen him in action in Iraq, Hayes had showed himself to be one of the most levelheaded and calm soldiers in my company. I had the sense that if he could lose it and hit a woman the way he had, any of us could lose it too.

Then something happened that haunts my dreams to this day. All the women were led back inside the house and our entire platoon was ordered to stand guard outside it. Four U.S. military men entered the house with the women. They closed the doors. We couldn't see anything through the windows.

I don't know who the military men were, or what unit they were from, but I can only conclude that they outranked us and were at least at the level of first lieutenant or above. That's because our own second lieutenant Joyce was there, and his presence did not deter them. He was the highest-ranking among the 43rd CEC soldiers at the house that day, and he would have had every right to question any person of his rank or lower who assumed control over our raid.

Normally, when we conducted a raid, we were in and out in thirty minutes or less. You never wanted to stay in one place for too long for fear of exposing yourself to mortar attacks. But our platoon was made to stand guard outside that house for about an hour. The women started shouting and screaming. The men stayed in there with them, behind closed doors. It went on and on and on.

Finally, the men came out and told us to get the hell out of there.

It struck me then that we, the American soldiers, were the terrorists. We were terrorizing Iraqis. Intimidating them. Beating them. Destroying their homes. Probably raping them. The ones we didn't kill had all the reasons in the world to become terrorists themselves. Given what we were doing to them, who could blame them for wanting to kill us, and all Americans? A sick realization lodged like a cancer in my gut. It grew and festered, and troubled me more with every passing day. We, the Americans, had become the terrorists in Iraq.

Just a few days later I used up yet another of my nine lives. Our platoon of three squads had been assigned to guard a public building used by local Iraqi officials. While we stood on guard duty, several rocket-propelled grenades came raining in on us. Three or four grenades bounced off the hatch of my armored personnel carrier. I was standing just a few feet away, but miraculously the grenades yet again failed to explode. We did what we always did in such circumstances, blasting away with our machine guns at the area where we imagined our enemies were hiding. We didn't stop to ask ourselves if any civilians were in the area; on orders from our commanders we just lit up the area with machine-gun fire. As always, we had no real idea where our true enemies were, or if we hit anybody with our return fire. A few moments later, we received orders to move out of the area, so we got on our three APCs and began traveling slowly back toward our compound.

About half a block later, as our three vehicles inched forward in formation, with mine at the back, we saw dozens of Iraqis assembling. I assumed that because our machine guns had finished lighting up al-Habbaniyah, people were coming out to see what had happened. Among the crowd was an older-looking man—perhaps in his forties or fifties—sitting in a chair near the side of the road. He wore the traditional white gown, and he was not armed.

As we approached, I saw the seated man raise his leg to bare the sole of his foot at us, a sign of disrespect. We all knew that this was the Iraqi equivalent of the middle finger—a clear "fuck you." As I watched, Sergeant Gurillo—perched atop an APC just ten feet ahead of mine—put the man in the sights of his semiautomatic rifle. Gurillo's rifle had a lever allowing it to be used as a machine gun or for firing single bursts, and Gurillo—a short, stocky guy who was known to us all for getting love letters from both his wife and his girlfriend—must have switched the lever to single-shot mode. He tipped the barrel of his rifle down ever so slightly, squeezed the trigger, and shot the man squarely in the foot.

The man tumbled off his chair and onto the ground and found himself immediately surrounded by a crowd growing louder and angrier by the moment.

My APC stopped rolling. So did the other two.

From his position in the first APC, Captain Bower radioed Sergeant Padilla, standing in front of me on top of our vehicle, as well as the sergeants on top of the other APCs.

Padilla told us that Bower was asking, through the radio, "Who shot that man?"

Nobody said anything.

Padilla told us that Bower repeated the question, so he relayed it to us one more time: "Did any one of you see who shot that man?"

Again, no soldier answered. Sergeants Padilla and Fadinetz had been with me on top of my APC, other soldiers were with Gurillo on his, and yet more soldiers were positioned on top of the first APC, but not a single person answered the question. I knew that I would get in more trouble for opening my mouth than for keeping it closed, so I did exactly the same thing as every other man in my platoon. I didn't say a word about what I had seen. As the lowest-ranking soldier in the three armored personnel carriers, I had no right to break the chain of command by speaking to Bower, and I knew better than to raise the matter later.

I feared that the crowd of people would riot and was relieved when our APCs began moving again and slowly rolled away.

Not long after Gurillo shot the man who dared to raise his foot at us, our commanding officer Captain Bower summoned us into the compound. He told us that a terrorist named Al Jawiri was holed up in a house and that we were going to smoke him out. He said our operation was called Task Force 26, and that it would involve elite soldiers from other military units. Rangers and marines would join this house raid, but the members of my squad were to go in first, as usual. Given the dangers, however, instead of blasting apart the door with C-4 explosives, Captain Bower instructed us to break down the door with our armored personnel carrier.

At this point, in the midst of our briefing, I lost it. I spoke up.

I said, "If you're using Task Force 26 with fancy military people, why do you need our squad? You say this is the house of a known terrorist, and you're sending us in first? Looks to me like you're sending us on a suicide mission."

The officer ignored my complaint. But that day I just couldn't control my mouth. I looked at Captain Bower and at First Sergeant Meyer standing with him and said, "If anything happens to any of us, there's a grenade waiting on you two!"

Sergeant Skillings, my squad leader at the time, tackled me. He took me outside and said, "What the hell are you doing? Do you know what kind of trouble you can get into for speaking like that?"

"That's how I feel," I said. "It's a damn suicide mission."

He said, "The only reason you're getting away with your loud mouth is that you know how to fix stuff and hook up our air conditioners."

We moved out to get ready for the raid. I traveled with my squad mates in our APC and, sure enough, we used it to ram through the door. We drove several feet into an open room, pulled back outside, stopped the vehicle, jumped out, and raced in with our weapons. Inside, we found two men on the floor: one sitting and one lying down. I could see that something was wrong. The two men were immobile. They were alive, and awake, and they showed no sign of injury. The men appeared to be in their forties or fifties. They both wore white robes. One had a mustache. But they remained utterly silent. Although we had just smashed into their home with an armored personnel carrier, they weren't getting off the floor or even turning their heads.

There was hardly any furniture in that house. There were no other people and no weapons or suspicious items. My squad mates jumped on the men, zipcuffed them, and started hollering at them to "get the fuck up" and "get the fuck out the door." The Iraqis didn't move. When my guys started kicking and punching, the Iraqi men didn't even try to block the blows.

"No!" I shouted. "Stop! There's something wrong here. Look at these men."

But the guys in my squad continued with the beating while all the other soldiers waited outside. As the minutes passed, I kept hollering at my squad mates to give up their beating and to leave the men alone. Finally, a medic ran in, waved a hand in front of their faces, got no reaction, and told us that the men were mentally handicapped. I gave my squad mates so much grief about beating up the two men that they got sick and tired of my bitching and sent me outside to pull perimeter.

These two Iraqis had been beaten up because they were handicapped and couldn't understand what we wanted them to do. But even once we understood that the men were handicapped, we showed no pity and took them away just like all the others we found in home raids.

It would have been a lot better if we had just left. While soldiers continued to ransack the house, in search of the terrorists that they would not find, I stood outside with the many soldiers assembled to take part in the raid.

Iraqi civilians began walking toward us. They wanted to see the house that had been rammed by our APC. Apache helicopters hovered in the air, and our APCs and tanks were lined up outside, and—with the additional military support—we had more firepower than I had ever seen in one place in Iraq. It was an eerie morning, the early dawn. There was light in the sky but the sun had not yet risen. I felt a cool breeze, and held my position guarding the corner of the house. Across the street, I noticed a man burning piles of what appeared to be Iraqi dinars.

"What's he doing?" I asked Sayeed, our interpreter.

"He is burning all his counterfeit money before you guys go over there and arrest him," Sayeed said.

Nobody else, however, was paying attention to the counterfeiter with his burning bills. The crowd continued to grow as people pressed forward to see the house we had rammed.

Suddenly, from another side of the house, a shot rang out. I heard shouting and over my walkie-talkie I could hear Sergeant Padilla speaking to another soldier in my squad.

"I thought she threw a grenade, and that's why I shot her," Padilla said.

I heard Padilla go on to say that he needed two other soldiers to push the crowd away from a body so that he could inspect it.

I had to stay put, holding my position for another thirty minutes, but finally as we were given authorization to leave I met with my squad mates near the APC, where there was a body on the ground. I saw that it was a young girl about ten years old. The girl Padilla said he had shot wore a school uniform and had blood on her skirt. I was struck by how little blood there was on the girl. I assumed that the bullet had entered her stomach. As the girl's body was being lifted into the bag and zipped up inside it, a soldier in my squad said that he had found no sign of a grenade or weapon on the girl. My squad mates lifted up the girl in the bag and set her down inside our APC. The rule was that if we killed somebody, we were responsible for policing the dead. That meant we had to get them into a body bag and take them back to our compound, where they would be kept until a relative came to claim them. When we left that scene, we took the girl's body with us and then left it at our compound in the shack used for storing the bodies of deceased Iraqis killed by our platoon or other platoons in my company.

I stood guard for many reasons during my months in Iraq. I guarded our own compounds. I guarded a green zone in the two weeks I spent there. I guarded a bank and a hospital and the perimeter of all the houses we raided. But the worst kind of guarding I was called upon to do, in Ramadi, Fallujah, al-Habbaniyah, and elsewhere, was to stand near the bodies of the Iraqi dead and watch as relatives came to claim them.

After the girl was killed in the aftermath of the raid on the home of the mentally disabled men, I guarded her body too. There were many other bodies waiting to be taken—sometimes as many as ten or twenty at a time—and it appeared to me that most of them came back with other platoons in my company. Our platoon had been responsible for a number of deaths, but it seemed to me that we were almost saintly in comparison to the other platoons, who often came back with numerous victims in body bags. Some even kept count of their individual killings. I was glad that I never had to enter an Iraqi's house with them.

I mostly avoided these men but sometimes overheard conversations when we were eating in the chow hall.

"I got my first one yesterday," one guy would say.

"So what?" somebody else would reply. "Today I got number five."

A day or two after the girl was shot, I was on guard duty with other soldiers at the front gate of our military compound, just a few feet from the shack with the dead bodies. A group of about fifteen Iraqi civilians—men, women, and children—left the road about a hundred yards away and began walking directly toward our gate. Iraqi civilians came to our compound only to pick up dead relatives, so I prepared myself for the inevitable discomfort. When they drew closer, I could see one old woman dressed in black; staring right through me. As she put one foot in front of the other, she would not take her eyes off me or release me from the hateful glare that seemed to be saying, "You are a monster. How could you do this? How could you kill the one I love?"

All I can remember about her, apart from the dark eyes radiating accusation and hatred, was that she was not veiled, had discolored sandals, and drew fearlessly toward me. She screamed at us in Arabic, and although I did not know exactly what she was saying I had no doubt that she blamed me for the death of the person she was coming to retrieve.

She continued to shout at us while others in her family dealt with an officer and the interpreter at the shack, and she wailed with her relatives as they carried a body in a short, four-foot-long bag. Tears filled my eyes. I wondered if she had come for the body of the little girl who had recently been killed. All I knew was that somebody she had loved had fallen from our bullets, and I felt nothing but shame and guilt as they walked away, carrying the dead with all the dignity they could muster.

When the old woman and her relatives left with the body, an officer from another platoon in the 3rd

Armored Cavalry Regiment—I do not remember his name or rank—ordered me to follow him into the compound. All I remember was that it was near the middle of a hot day and that the officer was thin, had a mustache, appeared to be in his thirties, and belonged to a tank unit in my regiment. And that he was very angry with me.

"What the hell is the matter with you, crying and all? You make us all look guilty when you show sympathy to the enemy."

He threatened to tell officers in my platoon that he had seen the tears in my eyes, and to make sure that I was disciplined. I was afraid my pay would be withheld or reduced and asked him if we could just deal with the matter then and there.

He gave me a written reprimand. I do not remember the exact wording, but it basically said that I had been found fraternizing with the enemy and that I had broken the rules of the American Uniform Code of Military Justice, which is a federal law governing military justice in the U.S. armed forces. I believe that he let the matter drop, because I never heard about this from my immediate commanders.

I continued to stand guard at the gate of our military compound about once every three days. Generally, I noticed that about one person or group of relatives came each day to pick up their dead. I could feel my spirit breaking little by little, allowing for the thing that many men cannot do. But I knew enough not to get caught again and to shield the tears from the men in my company.

★ ★ ★

Specialist Sykora was a friend of mine and one of the few in the platoon in whom I would confide my honest thoughts of the war. Although he had been in the army for years, he did not appear to believe in the war any more than I did. He had his wild side, though. He talked all the time about professional wrestling matches, and he had a thing about looking at dead bodies. One day, as I was walking past the shed used for storing the dead, I heard thumping inside. I opened the door, peered inside, and saw Sykora holding up a body in a zippered black bag. He raised it and dropped it like one might slam a wrestler in the ring, then picked up another body and slammed it down too.

I was nauseated and backed out of the shed immediately. I didn't like ratting on my squad mates, but it just didn't seem right to let Sykora keep it up.

I sought out Sergeant Fadinetz. "Sykora has gone nuts," I said. "He's inside the shed wrestling with bodies and tossing them every which way."

Fadinetz looked away and said quietly, "He needs to let out his aggression. Let him have his fun."

I had done my fair share of talking with Sykora, but after that point I stepped back from the friendship. He was just too much for me. I didn't see how anybody who had looked straight into the eyes of a grieving mother could entertain himself by wrestling with corpses.

★ ★ ★

There was a sergeant named Mike Meinen in the first platoon of my squad. He lived in Boise, Idaho, with his wife when he wasn't at war. A month or so earlier, he had handed out cigars to celebrate the birth of his daughter. I believe it was his first daughter, and I remember Meinen saying that he hadn't been able to get authorization to fly home to see her. He was a good fellow, and we would chat sometimes as we crossed paths on our way to and from the urinals at night.

In late August, while I was doing guard duty at the compound, Meinen and two others were patrolling the streets of al-Habbaniyah when they came under attack. Skillings told us that a rocket-propelled grenade of a type that the U.S. had given to Iraq during its war against Iran shot straight through the steel hatch of Meinen's APC. The grenade is made to penetrate steel and then explode, and it did its job to a T, slicing through the APC like a knife through soft butter and then splitting into shrapnel. The hot metal exploded inside the APC, cutting through everything it found. We Americans have good weapons, and I was told that we had used this one to fight in Vietnam. Meinen and two other men, Wyatt and Castro, were helpless against the exploding grenade. They escaped with their lives but not their legs.

The APC somehow made it back to our compound and we raced to the vehicle to help our buddies. A helicopter got there almost as fast as we did. As the three men were being evacuated for emergency care, I picked up Sergeant Meinen's leg and placed it next to him on the stretcher.

"Now I get to see my daughter," he said.

He and the others were whisked away. We heard later that all three survived and had been fitted with prosthetic legs, but in the aftermath of the incident a gloom fell over our squad.

My squad mates and I were ordered to clean the blood out of Meinen's APC, but we refused to do so. He was our friend and we felt that it would have been more appropriate for someone in another platoon—someone who didn't know him at all—to be assigned that task. Our squawking, for once, was heeded. Someone else was given the job. My squad mates and I did have to wipe the blood off the weapons. I cleaned Meinen's rifle. It too had been ripped apart by the grenade.

Some of the men in my company wanted to take revenge, to go out and kill as many Iraqis as they could. My own anger, however, was reserved for the president of the United States and the military commanders who had put us in this war in the first place. I could find no justification for our role in Iraq and could not think of a single positive thing we had done in the country. My friends had had their legs blown off, and what was it for? If my time came the next day and I was sent home in a body bag, would history see me as a hero or as an accomplice to evildoers? To my way of thinking, only a hugely positive result—such as preventing genocide or the proliferation of weapons of mass destruction—could justify all the sacrifices that Iraqis and Americans were making in this war. Yet several months into my participation in the

war, I saw no such positive results and no signs of them
either.

Not long after that, while guarding a weapons depot
in al-Habbaniyah, I confided in Specialist Sykora and Private Lewis, "If I get a chance to get away from here, I'm
never coming back."

"If you run they'll be all over your ass," Lewis said.

I gave it no more thought. Stuck in the middle of a
war zone, I found it too hard to think about what I would
do in America, or how life might work out for me.

A few days later, I asked Sergeant Jones about the point
of the war.

"There is no point, it's just your job," he said.

"But what's the justification for this war?"

"The justification is that you signed a contract and
you're told to be here."

"But when do I get to go home?" I said.

"Private," he said, "we can keep you here just as
long as we want, and we ain't never got to send you
home."

Soon after, while my squad mates and I patrolled
the streets in our APC, we passed under a thick grove of
palm trees.

"If you guys were fighting against me right now," I
said to Sergeant Fadinetz, "you would all be dead at this
very minute. I would have strung a mine up in those trees
and I would have been hiding right behind that big rock

over there, and the instant you people rolled under these trees I would have hit the switch. And you know what, Sergeant? Every one of you would have been dead."

To my surprise, the sergeant did not lecture me for speaking my mind. Softly, he told me, "I'd do the same thing if people invaded America."

That got me thinking. How would I react if foreigners invaded the United States and did just a tenth of the things that we had done to the Iraqi people? I would be right up there with the rebels and insurgents, using every bit of my cleverness to blow up the occupiers. I would dig a hole in my hometown in Oklahoma and rig mines in the trees and set them to blow up when the enemy passed below. I would lob all the mortars and rocket-propelled grenades I could buy. No doubt about it. If somebody blasted into my home and terrorized my family, I would become a force to be reckoned with. I would invent my own booby traps and come up with the most unexpected methods of mayhem. I would give the occupiers hell and keep at it until I was dead and gone, twice over.

7

al-Qa'im

AFTER LEAVING AL-HABBANIYAH, WE SPENT THE SECOND half of September in a so-called green zone. Located in the desert, hours from Baghdad, it was a fortified, protected oasis where thousands of American soldiers were sent to rest and relax. Outside the guarded gates, there was nothing but sand for miles in every direction—nothing, that is, except hundreds of Iraqi vendors lined up along the road. As we inched forward in a military traffic jam, the vendors walked among our vehicles, waving their arms and selling cigarettes, soda, ornamental knives, blankets, and clothes. I figured that every one of them had been affected by the war. We had bombed their cities, raided their houses, and most certainly killed at least some of their loved ones, but they knew we had money. I didn't imagine that the vendors had any other way to make a living, and I watched them as they swarmed our vehicles.

Sergeant Fadinetz and Specialist Sykora jumped off our armored personnel carrier to snatch up Persian rugs for a fraction of the price they would have fetched back home. Later, in a postal station inside the green zone, they would mail them home to their wives. Private Lewis spent $30 on an Iraqi military uniform, complete with stripes and awards. I wondered whom it had belonged to and what had happened to the man who had once worn it. I'm not a big spender, never have been. From the vendors, I bought a caffeinated drink called Red Bat as well as Mond and Mikado cigarettes. Most of the soldiers hated the cigarettes sold in Iraq, but I liked them just fine, and appreciated buying them for an eighth of the price of American cigarettes.

Endless rows of huge tents had been erected in the green zone, and we set up our cots in one of them. I spent my time sleeping, smoking, drinking pop, weight lifting, and hanging out with my buddies Lewis and Connor. I'm not much of a reader, but I stretched out on my cot and read *Into Thin Air* by Jon Krakauer, about a disastrous climbing expedition on Mount Everest. Krakauer brought such a keen eye to the fatally mismanaged climbing adventure that I found myself wishing he could have seen everything I had been through in Iraq, so that other Americans and I could read his analysis.

I also spoke to Brandi every day, a luxury I hadn't had since arriving in Iraq. There were a hundred telephones in one big room in the green zone, and thousands of soldiers lined up daily to use them. It often took an hour or two to get to a phone. Even when I climbed off my cot to call Brandi in the middle of the night, I still had to wait more than half an hour for the telephone. She reassured me that all was okay at home. Philip was a healthy, growing baby who slept through the nights. Adam no longer wore a cast and his broken arm had healed. Zackary did his best to help out at home and asked every day if I was still away in what he called "Sergeant World."

Brandi finally told me about the incident that had prompted Captain Bower to tell me I would not be promoted in rank because I had failed to "control my wife." She had argued with a soldier guarding the gate outside the Fort Carson military base. When she complained that the soldier picked her car for a detailed inspection, he called her a bitch. She jumped out and threatened to take a swing at him. From that point, the argument escalated. Nobody was hurt, but it created a fuss on the base. Somebody reported it to my captain in Iraq, who disciplined me as a result. On the telephone, Brandi said she was worried that I would be mad at her, but I just laughed. I loved my wife and had no desire to try to control her from any distance. I had seen too many grenades and mortars to worry about a tussle at Fort Carson. And I didn't care about not being promoted from private to specialist. I didn't want to be in this war anyway.

★ ★ ★

A few days after arriving in the green zone I called home with great news. Sergeant Skillings had told me that because I was low ranking and had a family, I would be next in line to go home on vacation. He didn't say when I would be flown back to the States, other than that it would happen eventually. Brandi was thrilled. The enthusiasm and affection in her voice helped me stay settled and relaxed during my time of rest. Apart from guard duty we had no work to do.

It was indeed something of a shock to move into quasi-civilian life in the green zone. Overnight, I felt like I was light-years away from what had been my daily life for the past five months. I had spent so little time sleeping, and so much time raiding, patrolling, guarding, and worrying when the next bullet or bomb was heading my way, that I found myself oddly uncomfortable in the safety and comfort of the green zone. I also found myself increasingly resentful, because most of the soldiers that I met from other companies told me that they had spent the bulk of their time right there in the green zone. I didn't even know who to be angry at: the soldiers themselves, for being able to eat and sleep well and call their loved ones every day, or my commanders, for putting the men in the 43rd Combat Engineer Company in such constant danger for nearly half a year in Iraq. I was so tired and messed up after the months of hard duty that I didn't even know what I wanted. Part of me longed to stay safe, sleep more, enjoy the decent sanitation, and call home every day. But another part of me—the part of me that has never known how to sit down and goof off—chafed at feeling so inactive.

There were many American women in the green zone. Some were soldiers and others officers. Sergeant Skillings warned us that punishment would be swift if we were caught having sex with any of them. Nonetheless, one day while I was waiting my turn outside a portable toilet—which seemed like a luxury in comparison to what I had known thus far in Iraq—a female private tapped me on the shoulder, smiled, and asked if I would like to sneak off with her for a fast fuck.

While my buddies snickered a few yards away, she said that they had told her I was a father of three.

"I want to get pregnant," she said. "It's the only way they'll let me go home."

I grinned but did not budge from my place in line. "Thanks, but no thanks," I said. "You ought to try Specialist Barrigan for that. He'll be game."

I pointed him out to her, and she left.

Barrigan thanked me the next morning.

"No problem," I said. The guys thought I was crazy for turning down the offer, but I told them I was a married man. "I've already had my fun," I told them, "and I don't want any trouble now."

A few days later I was propositioned again. This time, a lieutenant asked for sex. I refused again, and suspected that she was trying to entrap me. Word among soldiers in the green zone was that some officers tried to lure privates into sex, only to bust them for breaking the rules. There was no way I was falling for that. I didn't want anything getting in the way of my trip back home. I kept to myself, pumped iron every day, and kept lining up at the telephones so I could hear Brandi's voice. It was wonderful to be able to call home every day.

I coasted along knowing that I would eventually get home, but then I found out that it wouldn't be anytime soon. After two weeks in the green zone, Skillings told us all to pack up our things. We would be leaving the next day for a "red zone"—by which Skillings meant another dangerous assignment—on the Syrian border.

We all groaned. The guys in my platoon had been hoping to be sent home together for a break. We all felt we had earned it after months of hard duty and countless mortar attacks.

"Nobody is going home yet," Skillings said. "They need us for a tour of duty on the border. It's rough up there," he added. He told us that Americans had been meeting a lot of resistance near Syria. It would fall to us to stop terrorists from slipping over the border and into Iraq.

We loaded our armored personnel carriers onto fifteen flatbed trucks and spent two days crossing the desert. When you crawl at twenty miles an hour with all your hardware tied down on trucks, you feel a bit exposed—like a line of ants on a beach. Although our army helicopters occasionally swept by for protection, we didn't stop for a moment. When I had to pee, I did like the others and aimed off the side of the truck. When other needs arose, I just had to wait. A military convoy doesn't stop for bathroom breaks. At night, I sat on top of the APC, stretched out my legs, and looked up at the stars. Never had I seen constellations as bright as in the desert. Shooting stars made me think of falling mortars. Even looking at the most peaceful sight in the world, I could not get my mind off war.

I didn't know we were going to al-Qa'im until I saw a sign in English. It was a large but poor and dilapidated town of 150,000 people on the banks of the Euphrates. It seems the waters of that seventeen-hundred-mile river flowed everywhere I went in the country. Perhaps, I sometimes felt, the river was keeping an eye out for me. With all the dangers we faced, something must have helped keep me alive.

There had once been a uranium extraction plant in al-Qa'im, but our American army had bombed it to smithereens in 1991 during the Persian Gulf War. The main thing now, I was told, was to keep an eye on the border traffic and to shoot anybody who tried to slip into Iraq at night.

The entire 43rd Combat Engineer Company bunked in a warehouse by an old railroad station, a fifteen-minute drive east of town. The senior officers had their own rooms, but the rest of us—more than one hundred soldiers—slept together in one big room. Apart from our two-week break in the green zone, it was the first and the only

160

time in Iraq that my platoon mates and I slept in a building that had not already been destroyed by American bombs. It was loud, having a hundred men snoring all at once, but at least I didn't have to worry about the roof caving in.

After temperatures of around 120 degrees Fahrenheit in southern Iraq, the nights in al-Qa'im—perhaps 60 degrees or so—seemed bitterly cold. Gloves kept my fingers warm, and I wore a stocking cap on my head to keep off the chill and to ward off the sand. Storms blew in every few days, driving sand over me and all my possessions, even inside the warehouses. In the morning I would shake the layers of sand off my clothes and clean all the grit from my weapon.

In town, when I stood up on guard towers, I could see tanks blazing, jets racing, houses burning, and explosions in every direction. It looked like World War III out there.

Border duty took up most of our time in al-Qa'im, but we kept raiding houses as well. We took mortar fire and rocket-propelled grenades almost every day we worked at the border. They tended to fall on us in the late morning or early afternoon. As before, we could never see who was behind the attacks, but our men would shoot in what they hoped was the direction of the enemy. My weapon had stopped working and, failing to see the sense of it, I made no more efforts to have it fixed.

We often responded to mortar fire by raiding a house—any house—that seemed to be near the source of the attack. I was standing on a guard tower early one afternoon when another mortar attack erupted, followed by our own gunfire. When the battle ended our commander ordered us all into our armored personnel carriers so we could respond by raiding a house. Our three squads left the border, each in its own APC, made a quick turn, and came upon a middle-aged, gray-haired man walking at the side of the road. His hands were empty and nothing hung from his shoulders but a plain white robe.

From the first APC, a sergeant radioed to our vehicle, which was at the back. "Stop and apprehend that man," he called out to us. "He's in the area of enemy fire, so he's got to be guilty."

Specialist Barrigan, another squad mate, and I jumped out of our vehicle, grabbed the man, pulled him inside, and zipcuffed him.

Barrigan grabbed a billy club and started whacking the man on the head. When the man fell to his knees Barrigan continued to beat him in the ribs.

"I'll keep his mouth shut," Barrigan said as he pounded away; the man remained totally silent. He gave no indication that he could speak English.

I felt terrible for him, having to lie down and submit to that beating while soldiers kept their guns trained on him. When the man was dazed and motionless, Barrigan halted the beating. We returned to the border, dragged the man out of the vehicle, and brought him into an interrogation room.

He remained zipcuffed and silent. He sat on the floor bleeding from the back of the head. I felt sorry for the fellow and saw no reason for us to detain him. After an hour or so, while I stood outside guarding the door, an English-speaking Iraqi who worked at the border came into the room and spoke with Sergeant Padilla. When he addressed our victim in Arabic, the detainee spoke back angrily.

"Release this man," our interpreter said.

"Why?" Padilla asked.

"He works here at the border. He just finished his shift. He was walking home when you grabbed him."

Our men cut off the man's zipcuffs, opened the door, and sent him walking back home for the second time that day. He received no explanation or apology.

A few days later our young interpreter Sayeed left us just as quickly as he had joined our company months earlier. He came to say good-bye.

"Why are you leaving us?" I asked.

"Captain Bower told me that I can't go to America," he said.

I shook my head. I was not going to repeat now what I had been telling him all along. Sayeed said it wasn't worth staying any longer. Not for $20 a week. Not with the fact that Iraqis were threatening him for serving the Americans. And not after learning that all the promises made to him had been built out of thin air.

He extended his hand and I shook it warmly.

I thanked him for all the things he had brought us. I knew that a number of Iraqis had threatened to kill him for helping the American army, and I hoped that he managed to escape from Iraq before it was too late. I would never see him again, but I went on hoping that he and his relatives were safe.

My days at the border were long but straightforward. When the daily mortars fell on us, I took cover in a concrete shelter. As an American soldier, I could run into any building or shelter within reach when the attacks came our way. Although the mortars and grenades were aimed at us, they often fell near the drivers and passengers lined up in cars and semitrailer trucks waiting to cross over into Syria. Sooner or later, I was sure, travelers at the border would die—not because we killed them directly but because we drew fire in the very spot where they were trapped in their cars.

One of my jobs on the border was to inspect the cars and trucks leaving Iraq. People were allowed to take only five gallons of gas and five cartons of cigarettes out of Iraq and into Syria. My chief job was to find their extra stashes and confiscate them. Sometimes, when nobody was looking, I let the people go even when they were over the limit. I suspected that they were in desperate need of the gas and saw no good reason to deprive them of it.

Although my buddies and I worked as quickly as possible, we could do nothing about it when the Syrians decided to shut down their border. Sometimes, the Syrian border closed for hours or even an entire day. This created a massive buildup of vehicles. The drivers and passengers could do nothing but wait for the Syrians to open their gates again.

When the border shut down unexpectedly, I sometimes passed the time by smoking and chatting with men who climbed down from their trucks.

One man asked where I came from.

"Oklahoma," I said.

"Where is that?" he asked.

"In the south."

"The south?" he repeated, still confused.

I was going to explain where it was located, but the man raised his finger. He had something more pressing to ask.

"Your President Bush," he began. "Is he a good man?"

I turned to look in all directions. No American soldier was watching or was within earshot.

"He is a terrible president," I said. "If it was up to me, I'd be with my wife and kids back home."

The truck driver seemed shocked. I guess he had never thought that an American soldier would criticize his own leader.

"How long are the Americans going to be here?" he asked.

"Probably forever," I said.

"We've got nothing to eat and no money to buy anything," he said.

I didn't know what to say to the man, so all I could do was give him a cigarette. He looked at it and raised his eyebrows.

"Mikado?" he said. "Don't you have American cigarettes?"

"Sorry," I said. "Can't afford 'em on soldier's pay."

He shook my hand and returned to his truck. As I watched him close the door, it struck me that if he made it through the day and got across the border, he'd probably be back a week later to wait again in the very same place. The only way truck drivers could make a living was to keep carrying goods back and forth across the border, no matter how dangerous the task.

Not long after a mortar attack on the border, I saw a man open his truck door and stumble outside. He had a hand over a gaping wound in his stomach. I feared that his guts would spill out of him. I asked one of our medics to help him.

"I don't touch Iraqi blood," the medic said.

I ran to the man and gave him some of my bandages, but I have no way of knowing if he survived that accident or if he managed to get the shrapnel extracted.

During my six weeks of duty in al-Qa'im, I was sent four times after mortar attacks to check on truck drivers who had been caught in their vehicles. On two of these occasions, dead men fell out from behind the wheel when I opened the truck door. The other two times I had to pull the dead drivers out myself and lay them out on the ground. True, the Iraqis were killing their own people with those mortars. Still, I felt responsible. We had drawn the fire, and innocent people had caught it. Each time I pulled a dead man from his truck, I wondered whom he had last hugged on his way out the door and if his loved ones would ever find out what had happened to him.

One day Sergeant Skillings received a care package from his wife. Inside was one of the most treasured gifts of all—a two-pound tin of ground coffee. Skillings let us all share in the proceeds.

Sergeant Fadinetz and I frequently stood guard together on a tower at the border. The coffee sent by Skillings's wife helped us get through the all-night shifts on the tower. Fadinetz and I lugged a miniature, one-burner gas camping stove to the top of the tower, along with a percolator, the coffee, powdered cream, and packets of sugar. One night, while we stood sipping coffee, I heard a *zing zing zing* sound.

"What's that?" I asked.

"Dunno," Fadinetz said. "Good coffee, though."

I heard it again. *Zing zing zing.*

"Sounds like mosquitoes," I said.

I heard it again, looked behind me, and just a few feet away saw little explosions against the concrete wall.

"Get down," I shouted.

The next bullet grazed Fadinetz's helmet. We dove to the floor. The sergeant and I both had functional weapons on the tower—another soldier had lent me his for the night—but when we radioed our commanders we were told to hold our fire. That ticked me off. I thought of all the times our men had beaten, shot at, and even killed Iraqi civilians. But now, in a firefight with bullets whizzing around me, I had to crouch low and hold my fire. Perhaps it was just as well that I was made to lie low and stay out of the firefight. Although the shooting went on for an hour, we escaped without injury. I don't quite know how we managed to get through that night, but it didn't hurt to have had the coffee sent by the wife of a platoon mate. We had good coffee, which was a rare treat in Iraq, but I had paid with yet another of my nine lives.

I worked at the border along with Iraqi officials and police officers. I checked the dates on passports while the officials read the details. I was supposed to teach the Iraqis the finer arts of ripping apart a car to look for hidden weapons and other forbidden materials. To protect the infrastructure of Iraq, no one was allowed to take windows, lumber, or building supplies out of the country. I became pretty good at ferreting out hiding spots— under boards in trunks, behind false walls, and even inside spare tires and jacks—but all I found hidden was gasoline and cigarettes. I found no sign of weapons and arrested no terrorists. One friendly police officer invited me home to have a meal with his family. I had to refuse, but he would sometimes bring me bread, cooked slices of lamb, and fruit. Once in a while drivers at the border gave me dates, and I usually passed them along to the police officer.

We had clear instructions about what to do if we saw people trying to sneak into Iraq at night when the border was officially closed.

Nobody was allowed to cross into Iraq at that time, and if I happened to see someone trying to do so I was to shoot to kill.

One morning at about one a.m., while I stood guard on a tower at the border, I spotted a man sneaking into Iraq. He was about two hundred yards from the gates that opened during the day for traffic.

I didn't shoot at him myself; it was hardly necessary. The men in my platoon were stationed on various other towers at the border and they opened up with a barrage of fire. Some of the men climbed onto a Humvee, swung into place on a mounted, belt-fed, antiaircraft weapon consisting of two linked .50-caliber machine guns, and drilled hundreds of rounds at the trespasser. He somehow escaped the first blast of bullets and turned to run back into Syria. Still the men kept firing away and, after a blast of a weapon that normally would have been used against aircraft, the man's head exploded.

We were sent out to find the body. All I saw was blood and guts, and I turned away from the carnage. I had already seen enough of it in Iraq to last me for a lifetime.

In the photograph on the back cover of this book I am standing next to an Iraqi man. He wears the traditional white robe. His wrists have been zipcuffed, and a burlap sack covers his head. I am expelling smoke from a cigarette. This photo was taken in al-Qa'im, and I cannot say exactly what motivated me to pose for it. One of my squad mates took the photo. I don't think that any other soldiers posed with the prisoner, but most American soldiers did take photos when they had the opportunity. I did not beat the man, touch him, or threaten him. I never even saw his face. We picked him up from a little bungalow—serving as a miniature detention center—located at the headquarters of the second squadron of the 3rd Armored Cavalry Regiment. Two soldiers guarded the front door of the bungalow and another stood ready at the gate, where the prisoner was given over to my squad.

We were told to wait with him, just outside our armored personnel carrier, until we had authorization to take him to yet another location. There, I imagined, he would be held until he was driven somewhere else yet again, eventually arriving at some sort of major detention center.

I had no idea who he was, where he had come from, why he had been detained, or where he was being sent. This was typical of the few experiences I had with detainees. Except for the ones I helped grab and zipcuff during house raids, I never saw where the men had been first taken into custody or where they were going. And rarely was I in a position to witness how they were kept. One morning in Ramadi, while I was sitting on top of my armored personnel carrier outside a little house controlled by men from another platoon in the 3rd Armored Cavalry Regiment, I saw soldiers open the door and push a naked prisoner outside. The prisoner looked like he was about forty years old. One soldier kicked him as he stumbled out the door and into the light, and another soldier kicked him as he passed through the gate. The detainee was sent to stand in the middle of the street, and for an instant I wondered why he had been brought out like that. And then, in full view of passersby, the naked man defecated in the street. I turned my head guiltily, but not before I had witnessed his humiliation. He stood up and was kicked on his way back inside the building. I never saw him again, and I don't know what happened to him.

It would not be until much later, after I had deserted the army, that I heard of Abu Ghraib prison, west of Baghdad, or about the abuses of Iraqi prisoners at the hands of Americans, or about human rights violations at Guantánamo Bay in Cuba. While I was at war, I wondered where all the men that I helped arrest were taken, but at no time was I given any details or sent to any of the centers where they were held in large numbers. I only knew that we arrested every male over five feet tall that we found in our house raids and that I never saw one of them again in the neighborhoods we patrolled day in and day out.

In al-Qa'im, the detainee who was taken out of the bungalow and given over to my squad wore nothing but white boxer shorts and a rough sack over his head. We received no explanation as to why he was unclothed. Our orders were to wait with him at our armored personnel carrier until given authorization to drop him off with other soldiers. We gave him a white gown to put on, zipcuffed him, and kept him for thirty minutes until we were told to drive him a few miles to the drop-off point.

He didn't say anything during the time we held him. I don't even know if he spoke or understood English. Sergeant Fadinetz held a baseball bat ready, in case the man moved or attempted to resist, but he didn't use it, and I didn't see anybody lay a hand on the man or threaten him. Finally, we dropped him off with soldiers from a different company.

I regret posing for the photo with that man. It was a stupid thing to do. Even at the time, I derived no pleasure from his misery. I would have offered him a smoke if not for the bag on his head. As far as I was concerned, he was just one more Iraqi man who might never again see his family.

★ ★ ★

And now I come to the last story about my time in Iraq. I was still in al-Qa'im. I remained uninjured, despite all the bullets, mortars, and grenades that had been shot in my direction. As far as I knew, I had not killed any person in Iraq. I had not fired my M-249 since it had stopped working a month or two earlier. I had taken part in about two hundred house raids but had months earlier lost any belief in the cause. Most of my buddies felt the same way. The house raids were nothing but an excuse to insult, intimidate, and arrest Iraqis. They gave us a convenient target to vent our frustrations, never having any real enemies to kill in battle. For a time, the raids gave us an opportunity to beat people, steal their belongings, and destroy the things we didn't care to take. But I wasn't the only one who had let up on the beatings and the stealing as my conscience returned. For most of us, setting off C-4 explosives, ransacking houses, and zipcuffing teenagers and men provided a boost of adrenaline and excitement for a month or two at the most. As time went on, we found no weapons of mass destruction. We found no signs of terrorism. We found nothing but people whose lives would deteriorate, or end, simply for having met us face to face in their cars and their homes. Some of us had not even respected them in death.

And so, while I waited to find out exactly what day I would be allowed to return for a two-week vacation with my family, I found myself on duty as usual one day at the border in al-Qa'im. On this particular day, I was admitting people who were coming from Syria into Iraq, inspecting their passports and matching photos to faces. The travelers had little more than the clothes on their backs, and we usually let them in without delay.

I found myself speaking with a young girl. I don't recall her name or much about what she looked like, except that she was short, chubby, and wore a black dress. She had no veil over her face. She spoke English well. She told me she was thirteen and that she was an Iraqi. She said she had been in Syria when war broke out with the United States and was now returning to her family in Iraq. She was traveling alone, on foot, and had one suitcase. I checked the suitcase and found nothing but clothes.

I took her passport to an Iraqi official who was seated nearby in a shack. His job was to stamp the passports I brought him.

"What's this?" he asked.

"Just her passport," I said, waiting for the stamp.

"There's no stamp showing when she left Iraq," he said.

It didn't seem important, so I said nothing and waited for the stamp.

"How old is she?" he asked.

"Thirteen."

"And she is traveling alone?"

"Yes."

"Then she's a whore," he said.

My mouth fell open. I stared in shock. He hadn't even seen the girl.

"What are you going to do with her?" I asked.

"Turn her over to the Iraqi police," he said.

"Why don't you just let her go back to her family?"

"She's a whore," he said again and rose from his desk. "I'll turn her over to the police and we'll have fun tonight." He rose from his desk to go look at the girl.

When we returned to the girl, nausea swirled in my belly. An Iraqi police officer stood smiling beside her.

The border official told the girl that she was being turned over to the Iraqi police. Her eyes widened in terror. She didn't say a word, but I know exactly what her eyes pleaded as she looked my way: *I pray to God, please save me from these men.*

"Can't she just go back to Syria?" I said.

"Yes, Syria," the girl said.

The Iraqi police officer thrust his pelvis in a way that left no doubt about his intentions, gave the border official a big smile, and left with the girl.

Before he departed the border area where my platoon was working, I hurried to speak to the sergeant in charge that day and described the situation. I explained that the cop had rocked his hips in anticipation of what he would do with the girl, and that he and the border official were working together.

"They're going to rape her," I said. "Isn't there anything we can do?"

"It's their problem and none of our business," the sergeant told me.

I wanted to say more, but I also feared that my superiors would be happy for any excuse to punish me and deny me the opportunity to go home to my family. So I stayed silent, though I felt degraded by my own passivity and by that of my army.

By our sins of willful neglect, we were about to have a child's blood on our hands. I knew it was wrong then, and now I know exactly what the Geneva Conventions say about the protection of women and children in war:

"Women shall be the object of special respect and shall be protected in particular against rape, forced prostitution, and any other form of indecent assault."

"Children shall be the object of special respect and shall be protected against any form of indecent assault."

I knew how things were going to begin for that thirteen-year-old Iraqi girl, that day, but there was no telling how they would end. We had every means at our disposal to protect that girl. I say this because, in Iraq, sergeants and officers in my company generally behaved however they wanted in the presence of Iraqi civilians, employees, police officers, and border officials. In my opinion, it wouldn't have mattered in the slightest to my superiors what the Iraqis thought of our actions. If one of our officers or sergeants had chosen to intervene and protect the girl, no Iraqi working at the border would have been in a position to stop him. We were the ones with the ultimate authority at the border. Indeed, one of our roles at al-Qa'im was to teach the Iraqi border officials and police officers how to inspect a car, and to tell them what we would allow Iraqis to take out of their country and what we prohibited as export items. We were the occupiers and we controlled the border, but when it came to the fate of the thirteen-year-old girl who was about to be raped, we did nothing.

This is the last of my war stories. I dream of it still, and find myself waking and shouting out in the night. My own daughter, Anna, is not yet three years old. I can already imagine her questions, one day, and I do not look forward to them.

A few days later, as we were nearing the middle of November, Sergeant Skillings told me to pack my bags.

"You're going home in two days. Two weeks off. Enjoy it."

The guys in my squad were happy for me; they also knew that their turns for home leave were slowly inching forward.

Lewis asked me to bring him thermal underwear. Jones asked for a CD. Somebody gave me a letter to mail back home.

Sykora gave me a big hug. He said nothing, but by the look in his eyes he told me he knew I wasn't coming back.

The only person I dared to speak to was Connor, the Texan with whom I had bullshitted about football and southern life during our whole time in Iraq. That night, we sat on a flatbed railway car just outside our compound, while the other men in our squad were in their cots.

"This will be my last" was all I said. I didn't say "last day in Iraq." I didn't have to.

"Well, I'll be seeing you one day," Connor said.

Sergeant Jones came up to me just hours before I left.

"You're coming back, aren't you?" he said.

"Yes," I told him.

The truth was that although I didn't want to come back, I had no idea of just exactly what I was going to do, or where my life would take me next. All I knew, for sure, was that I would soon be back in Brandi's arms.

8

AWOL

Six and a half months earlier, getting into Iraq had been a slow process. After a long wait in Kuwait, I had taken a slow-moving trip across the desert in a military convoy. But on the way out, I was flown by helicopter from al-Qa'im to the same green zone (al-Asad) in the desert I had stayed in during the second half of September. After a few hours, I flew by helicopter to the Baghdad airport. There was nothing to do but wait, and that was a good thing because my mind was fried. Apart from two weeks of rest I hadn't slept more than an hour or two at a time for more than half a year at war. I had heard so many machine guns and mortars that I often found myself hard of hearingafter firefights. I could barely string three clear thoughts together. I knew only two things for sure: my own army had made me ashamed to be an American and I was finally going home to see my wife and children. I didn't know what I would tell my wife, but deep down seeds of worry began to take root in my gut. If I told Brandi that I was thinking about not returning to Iraq after the vacation, what would she say? Would she be furious? Would my lack of patriotism disgust her? Would she lose all respect for me? I wasn't sure if it was safe to tell her any of my worries, so on the long trip home I tried not to think about anything.

In the Baghdad airport, I ate an MRE, found a spot outside by an airplane hangar, rolled out my bag, and went to sleep. My next flight was on a C-130 to Kuwait, with about one hundred other soldiers. I knew none of them. I wore earplugs to drown out the noise of the engines and kept to myself.

Getting off the plane in Kuwait, we had to wait in line outside a security tent. Soldiers were not allowed to take weapons back home, and we were invited to leave guns and knives in an amnesty box before getting checked. I had dropped off my M-249 in al-Qa'im and I had already turned in my M-16 at the green zone.

Twenty officers checked the bags of soldiers who were traveling back home, but there were so many of us to process that it took two hours to move through the line. I saw one inspector fish a grenade out of a soldier's suitcase. No big deal was made of it. When I was finally next in line to have my bags inspected, I watched a soldier up ahead and to the left. An officer picked through his bag and even patted down the clothing. The officer shook open an extra pair of army pants, rifled through a pocket, and pulled out something thick.

"What the hell is this?" the officer said.

"An ear," the soldier said.

"Soldier, you want to take a human ear back to the United States?"

The soldier, who made no reply, was removed from the line and taken away.

When my turn came, a woman began to inspect my bag. She had heard the exchange about the ear and smiled at me and shook her head.

"I guess some people want to take some pretty dumb-assed things home," I said.

"You can't take all these cartons of cigarettes, soldier. Just two is the max."

"Okay," I said, "take 'em."

When she saw that I didn't mind, she said in a low voice, "You think that guy with the ear is bad. Last week, I caught someone trying to bring home a human arm." She was laughing as she talked about how she had to pull him from the line and leave him with a more senior officer. I didn't blame her for laughing. She must have seen her share of crazy stuff, and laughing probably helped her get through it.

"If he was trying to do that," I said, "he must have really lost it a long time ago."

She confiscated my cigarettes and let me go.

★ ★ ★

In the airport in Kuwait and on the long flight to Dublin, I noticed that most of the soldiers wore cleaned and pressed uniforms. I, however, was not exactly dressed for Sunday church. I wore the same dirty, bloodstained BDU (battle dress uniform) that had kept me clothed for six months in Iraq. I had an extra, cleaner uniform in my traveling bag, but I didn't want to put it on. I didn't want to dress up. I didn't want to look good. These were the clothes I had worn while at war, and I was disgusted by all the things I had been required to do. I didn't want to put a pretty face on things now, and I didn't care if my trousers and shirt hadn't been properly washed in six months.

On the flight to Ireland, an officer gave me a righteous look.

"Soldier, didn't you have a better uniform to wear home?"

"No I didn't, sir" was all I said.

I was tempted to tell the officer that I had been saving my second uniform for a special day. I had thought, during all my time in Iraq, that I would put it on when something truly good happened. But nothing good happened in my time at war, so I never put on the second uniform. Eventually wearing the same uniform day in and day out—and washing nothing but my underwear and socks—became my own private fashion statement. Given the things I had been made to do, why should I give a fuck about the way I looked?

The officer stared at the bloodstains on my trousers, but I didn't want to meet any roadblocks on my long journey home, so I kept my mouth shut and said nothing more.

When we landed in Dublin, it struck me that I had not had an ounce of alcohol for months. A sergeant stepped out of the airplane, took a look at me, and said, "Soldier, let's go get drunk."

We had only half an hour or so, but I slammed back eight beers as fast as I could. Nobody gave me a second look because just about every American soldier in the airport bar was keeping pace with me.

It takes about seven hours to fly from Dublin to Atlanta. I took every free drink they served on that flight and tried not to think about which was worse: beating up and killing the civilians of Iraq or refusing to do it any more and becoming a criminal.

Getting off the plane in Atlanta, I found Vietnam War veterans lined up on the tarmac to clap and shake our hands and to greet us as war heroes. I didn't want to shake any man's hand. What had I done that merited a handshake? I got away from the veterans as quickly as possible, drank while waiting for the next flight, drank en route to Dallas, and sat in the first bar I could find in the Dallas airport.

There, I didn't have to pay for a single drink. First, a man wearing cowboy gear from head to foot called to the barman, pointed to me, and said, "I'm paying for everything this soldier drinks."

He came to sit and talk with me and said he owned a ranch.

"How's it going over there in Iraq?" he asked.

"Have you been watching the news on TV?" I said.

"You bet," he said.

"Well, whatever they're showing, I can guaran-damn-tee you that it's not like that."

"How so?" he said.

I told him that innocent civilians were dying and that I didn't even think that I wanted to go back to it.

He gave me his name and telephone number and told me that if I ever went AWOL, I could come see him for a job on his ranch. I took his paper but knew I would never call him. People say all sorts of things they don't really mean.

When the cowboy left, a woman took his place as the buyer of my drinks. When I headed to the bar to clear my bill, she called out, "It's mine, I'm paying for it."

When I walked to the gate to fly the final leg home, I was so drunk that I forgot my bag in the bar. They had to page me to go back and get it. I doubt they would have let me on the flight had it not been for my soldier's uniform.

Brandi didn't recognize me until I walked right up to her.

"Oh my goodness, you look like a skeleton," she said. We threw our arms around each other. When we finally pulled back from the hug, she kept feeling my arms and my shoulders.

"Josh, there's nothing left on you," she said.

"Army food," I said, "isn't quite as good as yours."

"So does that mean you're going to start eating vegetables?"

"Give a soldier time to adjust," I said.

Brandi did not take a step without keeping her hand in mine or on my arm. "I guess you had a few drinks on the way home," she said with a smile.

"One or two," I said.

She took my arm firmly as we walked into the parking lot. She is a good woman, my wife. She didn't say one bad word to me about arriving home as drunk as a skunk. She just took my hand and led me home.

Zackary and Adam, who were five and three, dove into my arms. Philip, who was just over one, didn't know who I was. No matter. I spent the rest of the day loving on them all, and even Philip knew I was his father by the time he went to bed that night.

Back home in Fort Carson, my nightmares continued. I dreamed of decapitated heads, staring at me and calling out accusations. I dreamed of children dying. I dreamed of being in a firefight with no bullets left in my M-249.

I drank again a day or two after I returned and I blacked out. I don't remember what I did at the time, but Brandi told me later that I had screamed something about an attack and ripped the light fixtures out of the ceiling. Every day of that two-week holiday, even stone sober, I kept reaching for a gun that wasn't on my shoulder and felt naked without it. I couldn't stand in supermarket lines because I was afraid that someone would throw a grenade or bring out a knife. Brandi says that I was not the same man who had left just seven months earlier. I had no patience for crying children, couldn't walk outside without looking over my shoulder, couldn't get into bed without screaming in my sleep, could not stop mumbling about Iraq, and couldn't pay attention to a single household detail.

America felt like a dreamland. It seemed to me that not a soul in the country had the faintest clue about what I had been living through every day in Iraq. My buddies were in danger, and I thought about them constantly. But outside the military base, people in Colorado Springs carried on as usual, going to work, sporting events, malls, and movies. Walking about the city, a person visiting from another country would have had no idea that the United States was at war in Iraq. The long, slow buildup to Christmas seemed to be the only thing that excited the people of Colorado. But when I woke and when I went to bed, and when I ate and when I drank, I could not clear my mind of the places I had been: Ramadi, Fallujah, al-Habbaniyah, and al-Qa'im. I imagined that the house raids and traffic checks continued, and that American soldiers were still bombing, shooting, and beating Iraqi men, women, and children in their homes, cars, and streets.

I got drunk at a bar in Colorado Springs. Brandi says that I started shouting at her about how she and the children lived like royalty in comparison to the people of Iraq. Families over there had nothing to eat and nowhere to live, I hollered, and Brandi stared at me, wondering why I appeared to be blaming her.

"Just be thankful that our family doesn't have to live like that," Brandi said, pulling me from the bar. Deep down, I worried about just exactly how we would be living if I paid attention to the thoughts of escape swirling in my mind.

During the second week of my vacation, I settled down enough to help Brandi and the children move off the military base at Fort Carson and into a private apartment in Colorado Springs. It wasn't part of any plan to go AWOL or to run from the military. It was simply that Brandi hated living on the base and being surrounded by army life.

We spoke only once or twice about the possibility of going AWOL. I didn't say much. I only said that innocent people were dying at the hands of American soldiers and that I didn't want to go back to the war.

"If I run from duty, we would have to go far away," I said.

"Where would we go?" she asked.

"I don't know."

Brandi didn't get angry, and she didn't try to tell me what to do. But neither of us had clear ideas about what would happen if I didn't return to Iraq. If I ran from duty, where would we live? How would we eat? How would we take care of our three boys? All the time I had been in Iraq, Brandi had been receiving my $1,200 monthly check. But with rent, clothing, diapers, and food bills, my salary had been barely enough to keep the family going. We had no savings in the bank and less than $200 in our pockets.

My conscience told me that it was wrong to return to Iraq and to keep on doing things I knew to be wrong. But the very thought of going AWOL overwhelmed us. It was clear that we could never go home to our families. They had no means to support us or to protect us from the army officers who would most surely be lying in wait. We had nowhere to run and nobody to advise us, so we dropped the subject of my running from army duty before we had even discussed it seriously.

I spent the second half of the vacation unpacking boxes in our new apartment and sticking close to Brandi and the boys. They were the only people in the world I wanted to see. I barely went out and barely saw a soul. I made no contact with anyone at Fort Carson, and I did not even see or call the wives of the men in my company. I spoke with my mom and a few other relatives by phone but didn't tell them anything about my problems. In fact, I was so overwhelmed by daytime anxieties and bad dreams at night that I did not even know that President Bush came to speak at Fort Carson one day while I was huddled at home with my family.

Much later, when I learned of his visit, I went online to see what the president had said on November 24, 2003, to the troops at the Butts Army Airfield in Fort Carson.

"We're at war with terrorists who hate what we stand for: liberty, democracy, tolerance, and the rights and dignity of every person. We're a peaceful nation, yet we are prepared to confront any danger. We are fighting the terrorists in Iraq and Afghanistan and in other parts of the world so that we do not have to fight them on the streets of our cities. And we will win. In this war, America depends on our people in uniform to protect our freedom and to keep our country safe."

I can imagine this speech being televised live to the troops in Iraq. I can imagine returning at four in the morning to Saddam Hussein's bombed-out palace in Ramadi after raiding and ransacking a house and detaining its male occupants—even a fourteen-year-old boy who stood as tall as his father. If my buddies and I had sat in our bloodstained desert camouflage uniforms and watched a live broadcast of our president's speech, we would have thrown our rations at the TV screen. If our president stood for the rights and the dignity of every person, why had he allowed American soldiers to repeatedly abuse Iraqi civilians?

I was required to check in with U.S. Army officials in the Dallas airport on December 2, 2003. I didn't want to go back to Iraq, but Brandi and I saw no way around it. My wife was even more upset to see me leave after the two-week vacation than she had been when I'd left the first time, some seven months earlier. It would have been horrible to say good-bye under any circumstances. But it must have terrified her to see me like that—having lost a quarter of my weight and half of my mind—flying back to a war I did not believe in.

Brandi cried at the airport, but I did my best to hold back the tears. I could not have other soldiers seeing me like that.

I got on the airplane and flew south to Dallas, and I did not have one sip of beer. I was completely sober. I looked out the window at 32,000 feet. I felt that I had been out of my mind to get on that airplane and resolved to do something about it.

My stepfather, J. W. Barker, and my brother Tyler had arranged to drive from Oklahoma to see me off at the airport in Dallas. I met them when I got off the plane. Tyler gave me a big hug and J.W. shook my hand as if I was a war hero. J.W. went on so much about how I was serving my country and stomping out terrorism that I finally had to tell him to shut up. I didn't tell him what I had seen in Iraq. I just told him to be quiet.

While J.W. waited in a lounge, Tyler stood with me as I checked in at the U.S. Army counter at the Dallas airport.

"Your flight to Kuwait has been delayed two or three days," an officer told me. He began to give me information about a hotel room the army had arranged for me, but in my mind the switch had finally clicked. I was not going back to Iraq.

"It's okay," I said. "I'll stay with my brother in town."

The officer gave me details about the delayed flight,

but I didn't hear a thing he said. As Tyler and I walked away from the desk I barely looked at the papers I had been handed.

I called Brandi from the airport and told her that my flight had been delayed. We lamented about having been cheated of a few more days together. I promised to call her back that evening.

J.W., Tyler, and I drove to a restaurant. I ordered a steak.

"How about a beer?" J.W. asked.

"Just a Coke," I said.

J.W. raised his eyebrows. He could not drink any longer because of his liver transplant, but to him it didn't seem right for an off-duty soldier to pass up a drink. We didn't stay long at the restaurant. J.W. and Tyler wanted to hurry back to their hotel to catch an Oklahoma Sooners football game on TV. Funny: in Iraq, I had talked constantly with Connor about the Oklahoma Sooners, but now that I had returned from war I had completely lost interest in football and other sports. Once I had been a sports fanatic, but it spoke to me no longer. It would have been nice to be able to knock back a beer and lose myself in a few hours of televised sports, but three other things teemed in my brain: I wanted to hold my wife and children; I had the blood of men, women, and children on my hands; and I couldn't live with myself if I had to fight again in Iraq.

I called Brandi from the hotel room while Tyler and J.W. watched the Sooners game. Though my mind was made up, I couldn't tell J.W. I feared that if he heard I was planning to go AWOL he might turn me in to the military police at the airport. That night, after J.W. retired to his own room, I spoke privately to my brother.

"I'm not going back," I said.

"What do you mean?" Tyler asked.

"Just what I said. I'm not going back to Iraq."

"What's going on over there?" he asked. Tyler was nineteen at the time. Back home in Guthrie, he had a job with a landscaping company.

"I don't want to talk about it," I said. "It's fucked up. Innocent people are dying over there. It's not the war you think it is. I'm not going back."

"Well, what are you going to do?"

"Go back to Brandi and the kids."

"But what are you going to do when you get there?"

"I really don't know. But don't tell anybody, okay?"

"I'm your brother, Josh. I'm not going to say a word."

At six in the morning, I persuaded J.W. to drive me to the airport and to pay for my one-way flight back to Colorado Springs.

"Do you have authorization to go back home?" he said.

"Yes," I lied.

"Do you know when you have to be back?" he said.

"Yes."

I called home again from the Dallas airport and told my wife I was coming home. She didn't ask for an explanation and I was comforted that my wife would be happy to see me.

I caught the first flight to Colorado Springs, took Brandi into my arms again when I landed, and told her I was not going back to Iraq. That day, I called the office of the judge advocate general—a sort of military lawyer who is paid to advise soldiers in distress.

I didn't identify myself. I just said that I was thinking about not returning to duty in Iraq. He told me to think hard on the matter and to call him back the next day. When I called him back and explained that my conscience would not let me return to war, he became hostile: "Soldier, you can do one of two things. Either you get on that plane and get back to Iraq or you go to jail."

I hung up the telephone.

Brandi and I had to lie low until we could find some money. We put off paying every bill that came due—rent and everything else. We bought nothing but basic food for our family: bread, peanut butter, noodles, canned sauce, and milk. I stayed away from Fort Carson and knew it was a lucky stroke that we had moved off the base. The people at Fort Carson had no idea where I was, and I wasn't about to let them find me now. I stayed in our apartment as much as possible to avoid being seen on the streets. It helped that my entire company was at war in Iraq and that nobody on the base knew my face.

I stayed in hiding for close to two months in Colorado Springs. I needed a bit of money before we could leave. Early in January, I prepared my tax return, took it to an H&R Block office, and got a refund of about $500. That was what I had saved in taxes as a result of serving my country overseas. My mother sent us some money. Brandi had made a friend in Colorado Springs during my time at war, and they had quickly become close. Without her support and her money I don't think we ever could have made our escape.

Our Ford Aerostar van was falling apart, so I sold it to a neighbor for $100. I bought a broken-down, twenty-five-year-old Camaro for $700 from the son of an air force colonel. I put a minimal down payment on a rent-to-buy Compaq Presario laptop computer, took it with me, and never made another payment. Both Brandi and I were almost completely inexperienced with computers, but if we were going to go on the run, I knew that I would need to scout for information on the Internet. Using my military ID I arranged to rent a U-Haul for five days.

Finally, in early February 2004, Brandi, her friend, the children, and I took off. I drove the U-Haul with Philip in a car seat, and the women took the Camaro with Zackary and Adam. The Camaro ran, but that is about all I can say for it. It had holes in the floorboard and in the tailpipe. Exhaust spilled into the car, which forced them to drive with the windows down.

Our first stop was Louisville, Kentucky, but I felt nervous staying there because it was too close to the Fort Knox army base. So we didn't even spend the night in Kentucky. We drove to Trenton, New Jersey, but I was anxious and nervous and the city seemed too run-down for my liking. Still, run-down was exactly what we needed. I had come to the conclusion that a city in the northern states was where we had to hide. It had to be a city where nobody knew us. It had to offer countless places to get lost. It had to be a city that was rife with crime. It had to be a city with plenty of people passing through so that license plates from Colorado wouldn't attract attention. It had to be a city with so many thefts and murders that the police would have bigger things to worry about than a poor family in a broken-down Camaro. We picked Philadelphia and spent the first night in a highway rest stop outside of town.

I found a storage facility for all the stuff in our rental truck and abandoned the U-Haul in the parking lot of a suburban mall. Then I got on friendly terms with a security guard who kept watch over the highway rest stop where we slept in our car. Until we could start making money, we couldn't afford to pay for lodging. I didn't tell the security guard anything about my problems except that we were a family that had fallen on hard times. It's lucky for me that from time to time people have looked kindly on my family and me. He was an older black man, and he seemed to understand—without the need for explanation—that we could use a little help. The guard said he would let us camp out at the rest stop during his night shift but that we would have to be gone by seven in the morning.

Our friend found a job within two days as a waitress for a restaurant called the Dining Car. Brandi found a job just as quickly, also as a waitress, at the Olympia Café. It paid two bucks an hour plus tips. They pooled their slim earnings to keep us going. I spent my time watching the kids and being paranoid. It was not easy to keep an eye on my kids at a highway rest stop, or to move from rest stop to mall and back to another rest stop while Brandi was working. Somehow, I made it through enough days until we had money to pay for a room in the cheapest, sleaziest hotel we could find. We were given one room for $350 a week. All six of us slept in it together. We had to pay the money up front, but at least that kept me off the streets for a while.

While the women worked, I took care of the children in the hotel room. I made them stay quiet and played games with them. For entertainment, I let them play in the back parking lot, while I sat close by on some steps. But even that was a risk, and before I let the children outside I peered out every window for signs of men with crew cuts, four-door sedans with Colorado plates, or military stickers on cars or license plates. And I kept myself ready to run in case I spotted somebody on my trail. At all times, I had a knapsack within arm's reach, with a few clothes, a bit of food, some money, and maps of the city. I memorized bus and subway routes. And I never left any room without first peeking through the curtains.

I felt paranoid each time someone looked at me in the street and guilty about making fugitives out of my wife and my boys. The children spent most of their days locked inside hotel rooms, and I was sure that I had ruined their lives. Still, Brandi stuck with me. She never doubted me, never questioned my decision to run from military service, and never demanded detailed explanations. About Iraq, I said very little except that innocent people were dying and that I would not take part in victimizing civilians anymore. That was enough for Brandi, who would take my hand when I spoke. "If they are doing bad things, then you can't go back there" was all she said about it. I'm not sure if she understood that by helping me run she was doing far more than standing beside a fugitive husband. She was helping to keep me alive, and keeping me from mental collapse.

We changed hotels every month. A hotel needed certain qualities to be suitable for fugitives. It had to be cheap. It had to have staff who would take our money without asking for ID, who didn't care who stayed there, and wouldn't complain about six of us staying together in one room. They had to be willing to overlook the fact that we hooked up a microwave and a toaster oven wherever we went.

Our breakfasts consisted of cold cereal and milk. I'm addicted to coffee, but we didn't even have that. Lunches and dinners were always the same: bread, sandwich meat, peanut butter, and potatoes, which we bought in large, economy bags. We baked the potatoes in the microwave or sliced and toasted them in the tiny oven.

Most of the hotels offered Internet hookups, and I started punching words such as "AWOL" and "soldier needs help" into various search engines. For the longest time I found nothing at all. I saw details about the G.I. Rights Hotline, but I couldn't imagine that any American organization would be of help to me now. Still, I kept on believing that somebody, somewhere might be able to help us.

Not long after we arrived in Philadelphia, our friend told me that the owners of the Dining Car were looking for a dishwasher. I began working there at night, after Brandi had finished her restaurant shift. I changed my route every time I drove to work. I looked constantly in the rearview and side-view mirrors. Once or twice police officers followed my broken-down Camaro, but I had planned a strategy that worked in the short term: when I was being tailed, I drove into a wealthy neighborhood, parked in the driveway of a pleasant house, got out of the car, and walked to the door. I did my best to act like I belonged and the cops seemed to buy it, the few times they tailed me.

The dishwashing job paid about $7 an hour, and I kept it for almost two months. We continued living by the skin of our teeth, and when money was too tight to pay for a hotel room one week in advance, we returned to the highway rest stop with the sympathetic security guard. We could camp out in our car there from time to time, as long as we arrived after ten in the evening and left before seven in the morning. Rental apartments, no matter how cheap, were out of the question. We did not want to give our identification or our social security numbers to anyone, if it could be avoided.

It was lucky for me that no police ever pulled me over in the Camaro. The license plate stickers had expired and so had my driver's license. I had no automobile insurance. If anybody had punched my name into a police computer, I would have had handcuffs around my wrists in no time at all. Brandi, however, was pulled over twice, and once she was given a ticket for driving without an inspection sticker proving that the vehicle was mechanically worthy. Fortunately, I was not in the car on either of the occasions. When I heard about her encounters with the police, it made me even more determined to keep my head low. Every night, I watched the television news to see if the American government had begun some sort of crackdown on war deserters.

After a few months in Philadelphia, a job advertisement in the newspaper led me to try my luck at the Curtis Elevator Cab Company. I asked if they still needed a worker and was told to return the next day. In June 2004, I began working for $12 an hour—more money than I had ever earned in civilian life—making the insides of elevator cabs. Two brothers—Rich and Bob Andrews—ran the company and seemed to be happy with my work. I am a good worker, when I put my mind to it, and I do like to use my hands. For the Andrews brothers, I made the insides of elevators: the paneling, the railings, the boxes that held the buttons, and the light fixtures. I was employed as a general laborer and machinist: welding, using shearing machines and presses, and working with wood and glass. I made myself as useful as possible. I wanted to keep the job and make money and didn't want to have to look for another job until we knew what we were going to do in the long term. I had already chosen to give the brothers my real name and social security number. It was a calculated risk, but I knew that by working legally I would be entitled later to a tax refund because of my large family. But I sure didn't want to give my social security number to another employer. The more people who had it, the more likely it seemed that somebody would find me.

At the new job, the Andrews brothers didn't ask too many questions and I didn't offer many details about myself, other than that I had been a soldier in Iraq and that I had moved with my family from Oklahoma.

I soon had one more reason to keep my employers happy: by the summer of 2004, Brandi was four months pregnant with our fourth child and had decided to quit her job. We didn't have the money to send her to a doctor and we feared that any contact with the medical world could lead to my arrest. As a result, Brandi had no checkup until the seventh month of her pregnancy. Thankfully, she and the baby seemed healthy, so all we had to do was keep the children quiet as we stayed in hotels and remain working until we could find a way to safety. Our friend stayed in Philadelphia and kept working, and I don't believe we would have survived our long time in hiding without her friendship and support—particularly with babysitting and spotting us money. When we were broke, she never let us do without food and she never let us down. Twelve dollars an hour seemed like very good money to me, but it still wasn't enough to keep my family going.

My employers were kind to me. However, they were Republicans and we argued furiously about the presidential election in the fall of 2004.

"Of course you like Bush," I told them. "You guys are getting richer and richer."

We argued about Bush and we argued about the war in Iraq, but I did not tell them the things I had done or the things I had seen.

Sometimes human kindness comes at the most unexpected moments. Not long after President Bush was reelected, I told my bosses that my twenty-five-year-old Camaro had broken down so badly that even I couldn't fix it. When Rich and Bob said they had to step out to lunch they asked me to mind the shop. An hour or two later, they returned with a gift for me: a 1994 Buick Skylark, complete with new license plates. It was ten years old but better than any car I had owned before. It must have cost them a good two thousand dollars, and I would have liked to return the favor by staying a long time on the job. I accepted the gift because we needed it desperately, but I took it with a sense of guilt. It was dawning on me that to have a shot at a decent life we would have to leave the United States.

I continued to look online for information about war deserters and people who could help me. I had no experience with Internet searches but finally, after typing something like "war deserter needs help" into the Google search engine, I came across details about an American army deserter named Jeremy Hinzman. Apparently, Hinzman had left the United States and was applying for refugee status in Canada. If he was in Canada and hoping to find help, I figured there might be a chance for my family and me in that country too.

In October, using the address lotsofkeys@aol.com, I e-mailed Jeffry House, the Toronto lawyer who was representing Jeremy Hinzman. I didn't give him my name. For all I knew, he could have been an army agent posing as a lawyer to catch fugitives like me. I said I was a war deserter and asked if he could help. He gave me the e-mail address and telephone number of a Toronto group called the War Resisters Support Campaign. I called a woman there by the name of Michelle Robidoux and described my situation without giving my name. Michelle promised that her group would help me if I got across the border. At Brandi's urging, I repeated that I would be traveling with a wife and four children. Michelle reassured me that they would find a place for our whole family to stay. I didn't call her again for months and I hoped she wasn't setting a trap for me.

Christmas came and went and we had no money for presents for the boys or for ourselves. Thankfully, however, Brandi had been able to get free health coverage from the state of Pennsylvania for the last part of her pregnancy and her delivery. When the labor began, two days after Christmas, our friend stayed with our three boys while I drove Brandi to the hospital. I had always wanted to have a girl, but now I could barely think about it because I was terrified that I would be nabbed in the hospital delivery room. While I looked out windows for government cars in the hospital parking lot, Brandi had our baby after four hours of labor. We had a girl and named her Anna. She nearly died on her first day. She had aspirated meconium in the womb and developed pneumonia after she was born. On

December 27—the same day that she came into the world—Anna had to be rushed to another hospital for emergency care. But Anna recovered and we were able to take her back to our hotel three weeks later. As poor as we were, it seemed a miraculous gift to have a baby daughter. It struck me, as we drove back to the hotel where our friend was camped out again with our boys, that the gift of a daughter might never have been mine if I had returned to fight again in Iraq. Rather than helping to create a new life, I might have ended that of somebody else.

It seemed unbelievably risky to leave the United States and enter a foreign country with nothing more to go on than a promise that a stranger had made over the telephone. But staying in my own country was even more dangerous. If I stayed, something would eventually go wrong and I would get caught. And if I stayed I was condemning my wife and my children to a never-ending life on the run. I finally concluded that going to Canada offered the only real chance for me to avoid going back to Iraq or serving time behind bars. I knew almost nothing about Canada. I had heard that Canadians spoke English and French, but I didn't even know the name of Paul Martin, who was prime minister at the time.

I knew we needed to have some money in case things went terribly wrong for us in the new country. And the only way I knew then to get money was to file a tax return in early 2005, knowing I was likely to get a

big refund. It was a risky thing to do. But I had to hope
that the IRS and the U.S. Army had bigger fish than me
to fry and that, even if they did decide to put their heads
together and nail me, it would take them some time to
get around to it.

As soon as I got the necessary forms from my em-
ployer, I took my tax return to an H&R Block office in
Philadelphia. I had to give an address, so I gave that of the
hotel where we had been staying. As a precaution, we then
moved into an apartment our friend had rented so that we
could no longer be found at the address on the tax return.
The six of us stayed in a one-bedroom apartment. It wasn't
comfortable, but we lived better than most Iraqis under
American occupation. We had all the water we needed and
no bombs were falling through our roof nor soldiers busting down our door.

In March, I received a federal check for about
$3,000. It was the most money I had ever had in my life,
and it would have to be enough for our trip to Canada. I
gave our friend the car we had been using because it wasn't
big enough for a family of six. To replace the Buick Skylark, I bought a 1992 Dodge Caravan—with 202,000
miles on the odometer—for $600.

I called Michelle Robidoux one last time at the War
Resisters Support Campaign office in Toronto. Michelle
warned us that a border official might ask for details about
where we were staying in Canada. In that case, she said that
we were to give the name, address, and telephone number

of a person in Toronto who was a friend of the war resisters movement. Michelle also instructed us to say that we
were coming to Toronto to see the musical *Mamma Mia!*
She gave me the name and address of a man and woman
who would let us stay for free in their home. I asked once
more if she knew that I was coming with a wife and four
children. Yes, Michelle said, that would not be a problem.
I then told her the day that I would be entering Canada,
and I told her that I would do so at the border at Buffalo.
But I was lying. I did not cross that day, and I did not take
that crossing, because I felt there was a chance I was being
set up by U.S. Army officials. Two days after I said I was
coming, we drove to the border at Niagara Falls, New York,
with Brandi at the wheel. My driver's license had expired
but hers was up to date.

Sucking up the courage to drive to the border of
my own country was the hardest thing I had ever done.
It would have been easier in some ways to go back to war
and serve my time. It would have caused me a lot less
stress to sit in a jail cell. But I didn't want to participate
in an unjust war, and I didn't believe it was right that I
should become a prisoner in my own country for refusing to act like a criminal in Iraq. I felt that the only right
choice was to move forward, and I did so with my wife
and my children beside me.

I could hardly breathe during the drive to the border. Brandi and I cooked up an insane plan about how, if
it looked like officials were going to arrest me, she would

try to distract them and give me an opportunity to run away or even jump from a bridge. But in my heart I knew there was no escape in my own country. This was the moment of truth. Either I would get out or I would be arrested. And if I was arrested there was always the chance that Brandi would be arrested too for assisting in my escape. And then what would happen to our children? I also knew that if we somehow managed to make it across the border with no passports and no up-to-date identification, I would never again be able to return to my country.

Brandi and I had already lost touch with our families. With the exception of my brother and my mother, most of our relatives saw me as a traitor and a coward. From what I'd heard, Brandi's family felt that I had ruined her life and turned us all into criminals. We had just said good-bye to our one true friend, who would finally be returning to her home after over a year away.

We arrived at the border around the noon hour, hoping that the officials would be in a hurry processing traffic and unlikely to take a close look at us.

"Citizenship?" the border guard asked.

"American," Brandi said.

"What kind of work do you do?"

"I'm a waitress and my husband is a welder."

"Where are you heading?"

"Toronto."

"What's going on there?"

"We're going to visit a friend for the weekend," Brandi said.

"Why do you have all that stuff along with you?"

"You know what it's like, traveling with kids," Brandi said.

"Have a nice visit," he said.

We said good-bye to our country and drove into Canada.

Epilogue

My grandfather Elmer Porter had a blackout recently. It was the summer of 2006, and his tour of duty as an American soldier in the Korean War had finished more than half a century earlier. He had retired long ago from his job as a mechanic at Tinker Air Force Base in Oklahoma and was living quietly on his forty-acre farm. One day, for no particular reason, he thought he was under attack. He thrashed and fought to the limit of his strength, and when he snapped out if it he discovered that he had trashed his own living room.

A Canadian psychiatrist told me that you never truly emerge from post-traumatic stress disorder, that you simply learn to live with it.

There are certain things that I avoid these days, such as alcohol and crowds, because I fear they will trigger more of my own blackouts. I know that thousands of American soldiers have abused drugs or committed suicide after returning home from war. It would be easy to follow in the steps of many in my own family and drown my shame and my sorrows in alcohol. Alcohol, however, could lead to the very problem of suicidal depression that has plagued vets for generations. I won't go down that road. I have a wife and four children who need me, and they are the single greatest reason why I want to stay alive and to lead a good life. As for the big city, well, I remain an Oklahoma boy at heart, and I like wide-open spaces, so I have fled Toronto and settled in the Canadian prairies.

I am not a man to lead countries or direct armies. I have my high school diploma from Guthrie, Oklahoma, and if I am lucky I will move one day with my family closer to a school where I can learn the trade of welding.

When I was still a soldier in Iraq, I heard that many of the sappers who were discharged from American military service went on to defuse mines in war-torn lands such as the former Yugoslavia. I think of the countless children who have died, or who have had to learn to go on living with missing limbs, because they stepped on a mine—sometimes years after war officially ended in their country. I think of all the land that can't be trespassed on or safely used simply because men who passed that way earlier were trying to kill one another. Mines do more than endanger people; they also poison their future. In my military training in Missouri and Colorado, I loved the challenge of setting and stripping a mine and learned to work with nimble fingers under pressure. But I sure wouldn't want to live anywhere near the place where a soldier like me had been busy at work. A lot of ingenuity goes into killing, and it seems to me now a sad waste of money and intelligence. Somebody has to clear minefields in countries where men have stopped fighting, but I am not in any shape to join the brave sappers who have taken on that work.

War took all the fun and the challenge out of guns and bombs for me. Given what I've seen of what guns and bombs do to people, I can't go back to them now and hang on to my sanity. These days, my personal and family ambitions are simple yet hard to obtain. I would like to be able to dream without nightmares about the people I traumatized in Iraq. I would like to have a few acres of land and make a steady living as a welder so that my children can grow up decently clothed and properly fed. I want to be a good man to my wife, who gave up her family and her country to support me in my flight from the war in Iraq.

I grew up drinking and fighting and placing beer bottles on my rifle range, and I rarely stopped to imagine life outside Oklahoma. I expected to grow old and die in the very place I was born. When I first met Brandi, I told her that I loved Guthrie and never wanted to leave it. I was not a political man. In fact, when I was a child and a teenage boy the most political thought that entered my head came from the words of my grandfather Elmer, who told me that in the United States, the Republican Party stood for the rich and that everyone else should vote for the Democrats.

I'm glad I had Elmer in my life. A lot of men moved in with my mother and out again, and I still cringe at the memory of her body being flung against the wall of our two-bedroom trailer. They say that you end up doing what the people in your family have done. I'm determined that this will not be true for me. No way. My grandfather was the only person I ever knew who told me that no man had any business beating his wife. I'm glad I had that one good voice in my childhood. His is the voice I have chosen to hear.

I like to think it was my grandfather's voice—the voice of right and wrong—that woke me from the long sleep I fell into during military training and the first months of war.

There is no excuse for the things I did in Iraq, or for the beatings I delivered—on orders from my drill sergeant—while training with the American army in Missouri. Looking back, I am filled with shame that I beat up other recruits just to please my drill sergeant. I am disgusted to think that I tried to break a man's ribs by swinging away with a soap-filled sock just because he resisted an order. In the end, the man I beat up was the one with the brains. He had the courage to stand up to an institution bent on breaking him and recasting him as a killer, and I heard in the end he managed to get out of the military. That would be good for him, and good for Iraq.

My commanders had told me that it is army first, God second, and family third, but I'll never buy into that way of thinking again.

If you have beaten or killed an innocent person, and if there remains a shred of conscience in your heart, you will not likely avoid anguish by saying you were only following orders. We each have to find what we believe to be the right way to live. When we prosecute an unjust war, or commit immoral acts in any war at all, the first victims are the people who were unfortunate enough to fall into our hands. The second victims are ourselves. We damage ourselves each time we violate our own true beliefs, and the wrongs we commit weigh on our shoulders to the grave.

I cannot say exactly what would have happened if I had refused to blow apart the homes of Iraqis; if I had refused to send every male over five feet in height to American detention centers. I imagine that I would have been humiliated and punished by my superiors. I may have been beaten. Perhaps they would have sent me home to prison or disgrace. But if every single soldier in the American army had refused to blow off the doors of houses in the residential streets of Iraq, I will bet you that the generals and colonels and captains who commanded us—and our president and commander in chief, George W. Bush—would not have volunteered for the job.

I am ashamed of what I did in Iraq, and of all the ways that innocent civilians suffered or died at our hands. The fact that I was only following orders does not lessen my discomfort or ease my nightmares. After I came across the four decapitated bodies by the side of the road in Ramadi, and saw soldiers in my own army kicking the heads for their own amusement, I began to dream of the incident and of the rolling heads. Though I had arrived after the murder, the very fact that I saw the results and was part of the machine that committed the act weighed on my soul and weighs on it still.

I believe some people will say that Americans faced a nasty, unconventional war in Iraq, and that we had no choice but to take the war to our enemy in unconventional ways. My feeling is that we lacked the information, the skill, and the experience to find our true enemies in Iraq. We liked to think of the Iraqi fighters as inhuman and stupid, but the fact of the matter is, they outfoxed the American military wherever I went in Iraq. They threw mortars and grenades our way and we never even saw them running away. My fellow combatants and I never once put an armed enemy in our gun sights. They were on the run and gone while we were still diving for cover against flying shrapnel. We fought back by lashing out at civilians who had no means to defend themselves. It seemed the only way we could fight back—but it was wrong.

I don't think that senior American military commanders made soldiers raid thousands of civilian houses because they truly believed we would nab terrorists or find weapons of mass destruction. I think they did it to punish and intimidate the Iraqi people. In the eyes of the American military, Iraqis were not people at all—they were terrorists, suicide bombers, sand niggers, and ragheads. We had to think of them as less than human in order to keep doing the things we did. We were taught to think of Iraqis in degrading ways during military training, and those attitudes crossed the oceans with us when we flew into battle.

The Geneva Conventions are international agreements—which the United States and almost all other nations have signed—that aim to limit the barbarity of war by protecting civilians and prisoners of war. Basically, they set out the dos and don'ts of war. The most significant don'ts are not hard to imagine: soldiers are not to steal from, beat, torture, rape, or kill civilians or prisoners of war. I won't go on and on about all of the Geneva Conventions violated in Iraq, but I do want to quote one in particular: "Parties to the conflict shall at all times distinguish between the civilian population and combatants and between civilian objects and military objectives and accordingly shall direct their operations only against military objectives."

I would not have deserted the U.S. Army, left my country, or chosen to speak out against the war in Iraq if American soldiers in my company had limited themselves to fighting enemy combatants. I left the war in Iraq because the American army made no distinction between the two. We were taught in training to see all Iraqis as enemies and we were encouraged to keep thinking this way, and acting accordingly, from the first day that the 43rd Combat Engineer Company pulled into the city of Ramadi.

I had not read about the Geneva Conventions before setting foot in Iraq. But all I had to do was think of the teachings of my own grandfather at home to know that what we were doing there was wrong. I hold my army in judgment for the repeated abuses of Iraqi civilians, but I hold myself in judgment too.

When Nazi war criminals were brought to justice at the Nuremberg trials in 1945–46, an important principle was established: claiming that one was just following the orders of a superior does not relieve one from the responsibilities of international law, provided that a moral choice was possible.

I am responsible for the things I did. And my commanders were even more responsible for putting us there and ordering us to do the things we did. It was bad enough that we had nobody monitoring our behavior in Iraq or holding us accountable for it. But the situation was made worse because we had tacit approval from our commanders to shoot first and ask questions later. If a soldier beat up or shot somebody, all he had to say—if he said anything at all—was that he felt threatened. As a result, our behavior at war was completely unchecked. That's why it was possible for American soldiers to decapitate Iraqis by means of machine-gun fire and then use their heads as objects of play.

In Iraq, I did not witness the equivalent of the American massacre of hundreds of unarmed Vietnamese citizens in the hamlet of My Lai in 1968—for which I am glad. I hope that American soldiers have not committed such staggering atrocities there. Instead, I saw a steady stream of abuse and individual killing—a beating here, a shot there. Collectively, however, these incidents added up. Sometimes I wonder how the world might change if with my own eyes—and perhaps with a movie camera on my shoulder—I had witnessed every civilian beating and murder that American soldiers have carried out in Iraq. I wonder what would happen if every atrocity were compressed into the same day and the same city, still with my eyes watching and my camera at the ready. Then, I suspect that the total number of victims would shock and astonish Americans just as profoundly as did the discovery of the My Lai massacre. Alone, I cannot paint such a picture, but I know what I have seen. I shudder to imagine the thousands upon thousands of Iraqi families who this very day are struggling still with the loss of a loved one who died, completely innocently, at American hands.

When American soldiers beat up, stole from, and killed Iraqi civilians during my six and a half months at war, I saw them do so with complete impunity. We were far more than soldiers fighting enemy insurgents. To the civilians of Iraq, we became police officers, prosecutors, jailors, and executioners. We claimed to be bringing democracy and good order to the people of Iraq, but all we brought were hate and destruction. The only thing we gave to the people of Iraq was a reason to despise us—and perhaps to want to kill us—for generations to come.

In my last months in Iraq, I met soldiers who felt the same way I did about the abuses we were dishing out day after day. For the most part we kept our mouths shut. We lived in a military culture that had already taught us that although we could get away with beating or even killing Iraqi civilians, punishment would be swift and harsh if we even questioned our commanders. By remaining silent, we made it possible for the abuses to continue. I do not know what all of the other companies of the American armed forces were doing while I was busy with the 43rd Combat Engineer Company. But since coming to Canada I have read accounts of convictions against members of my 3rd Armored Cavalry Regiment for the abuse of Iraqi civilians and the torture and murder of at least one prisoner of war. I never met the people who have been convicted, and I did not know of them when I was at war. Sadly, it does not surprise me that they belonged to the 3rd Armored Cavalry Regiment.

On November 26, 2003—just two weeks after I'd left Iraq—an Iraqi major general by the name of Abed Hamed Mowhoush died while being interrogated and tortured by members of the 3rd Armored Cavalry Regiment. Mowhoush had surrendered to American soldiers in my regiment in a vain attempt to obtain the release of two of his sons who had been captured earlier. Water was poured down his throat in order to choke him. He was also stuffed headfirst into a sleeping bag and wrapped in electrical cord during one interrogation. Subsequently, a U.S. military court convicted Chief Warrant Officer Lewis Welshofer—

also from Fort Carson, by the way—of negligent homicide in Mowhoush's death. Welshofer's only punishment was a reprimand and a $6,000 fine. I wonder what punishment a court would have meted out if the victim had been an American citizen. And Captain Shawn Martin—who, like Welshofer, was part of the 3rd ACR—was charged on accusations that he had used a pistol, his fists, and a baseball bat that he called his "Iraqi beater" to threaten and abuse civilians and his own troops in an Iraqi town by the name of Rutbah. Martin was eventually convicted of three counts of assault against Iraqi civilians. His lawyer claimed that Martin was a good soldier who was authorized to use tough techniques. Martin's punishment: a $12,000 fine and forty-five days behind bars.

After I left Iraq and came to Canada, it came to light that American soldiers had been humiliating and abusing prisoners at the Abu Ghraib prison west of Baghdad. Two soldiers—neither of them members of the 3rd ACR—were jailed for taking photographs of prisoners in forced poses. When I was in Iraq I had no idea where our troops sent all the men and boys I detained in house raids. Every single male we found who was over five feet tall was zipcuffed, head-bagged, and tossed onto the back of the five-ton truck waiting dutifully outside each house we raided, ransacked, and plundered. I still shake my head in shame and wonderment when I think of the Iraqi man who had the guts to shout out in anger—as he was being seized by my squad mates—when he saw me stealing one hundred dollars in American bills that I had found in his house.

"Why are you taking that money? It's not yours."

I kept the money, and for a good while I held the attitude that Iraqis had no rights in their own country. It was an attitude I had picked up from my commanders, and it took me an embarrassingly long period of time before I began to question and then reject it.

When I fled to Canada, I was required to make a deposition to the Canadian Immigration and Refugee Board, stating why I was seeking official refugee status. In this book, I have addressed all the facts set out in that deposition, and have written for the first time about a number of other incidents that I also witnessed in Iraq. However, there are two details in the deposition that I wish to correct, for the record.

The first has to do with the killing of a child in al-Habbaniyah shortly after my platoon raided a home inhabited by two disabled men. The deposition says that the victim was a boy. That is an error. The child was a girl. I am not sure how it came to be recorded incorrectly in the deposition, but I remember all too well that young girl in her school uniform, and I always will.

The second detail relates to the number of houses my platoon mates and I raided in Iraq. The deposition says that I conducted about 75 raids. At the time that I prepared the deposition, I was anxious to avoid any possibility of overstating the number of raids. However, after making that first statement, I have had many more months to reflect on the matter and to do a tally of our raids. I now realize that two hundred raids is a far more accurate figure, and I believe that this estimate is still conservative.

If we detained an average of one male per home—and that would be a conservative estimate—that means that the men in my squad alone sent two hundred men into detention centers and prisons. I can only imagine that some of them ended up at Abu Ghraib.

Some people will say that the terrible things I have described seeing in Iraq were exceptions to the rule. This might be comforting, but it would also be naive to think so. Because I saw fundamental violations of basic human rights every day or two for six and a half months in Iraq, and since I never saw one soldier or officer criticized or disciplined for carrying out such violations, I tend to fear the opposite. I fear, and believe, that what I saw was only the tip of the iceberg in Iraq. I know that on two occasions when I did encounter other military companies in Iraq, I also witnessed the murder of Iraqis I believed to be civilians. I am thinking of members of the 82nd Airborne Division who shot and killed twelve civilians in Fallujah. And I am thinking of the members of the Florida National Guard who shot up four Iraqis so mercilessly. "We fucking lost it, we just fucking lost it," one American soldier of the guard hollered when I came upon him and his buddies as they stood near the decapitated bodies. By a fluke of timing, I had caught him in a moment of complete honesty. He said it when the heads had just been severed and the blood was still fresh. He said it before he knew enough to shut his mouth. And as far as I could tell, he was speaking the ugly truth.

In our military training and in our daily experiences at war, American soldiers were taught to show no regard for the lives of Iraqis—not even for civilians. This will go on until one of two things happens: the people of America no longer tolerate it or the people of Iraq find their own ways to strike back at us. In my opinion, the September 11, 2001, attacks on the United States were cowardly and despicable crimes. On that day, the terrorists had no right to take the lives of American civilians. But I fear that our own behavior in Iraq has invited more of the same. The young Iraqis who survive our raids, abuse, and detentions have all the motivation they need to seek revenge. I am not looking forward to the day they get organized. Whenever I remember standing with three hundred military trainees in Missouri shouting, "Kill the sand niggers" as loud as we could while stabbing and slashing with our bayonets at straw dummies, I say to myself that I hope the Iraqis who survive our war prove to be more civilized than we were.

When I was in high school, I would have scoffed if one of my friends had predicted that I would one day become an antiwar activist. If anyone had suggested that newspapers, magazines, and documentary films in North America, Europe, and Japan would be examining my role in the war in Iraq and talking about why I had run from it, I would have thought that they were out of their mind. I grew up a patriot, I entered the American army as a patriot, and I commenced duties raiding homes, patrolling streets, and checking cars in Iraq as a patriot. I hated to read and write as a child, but if somebody had forced me to predict—maybe in my school yearbook—what would happen in my future, I would have written that I'd have a family, believe in my country and my government, and become a workingman in Guthrie, Oklahoma. Perhaps I would have become a mechanic, or a welder if I was lucky.

Going off to war in Iraq and then going AWOL— first in my own country and then fleeing to Canada— forced me to give up many things. I had to give up my innocent and unexamined belief that my country and my army were a force only for good in the world. I had to give up my assumptions that leaders of my own country would speak the truth when they spoke to me. I learned the hard way that it was not true that I could sign up for the military and choose to become a bridge builder in the continental United States. The way the military reeled in the other recruits and me—many black and Latino, and all poor—I now call the poverty draft. It was not true that Saddam Hussein possessed weapons of mass destruction. And it was not true that every man, woman, and child in Iraq was an evil terrorist who deserved American hatred, bombs, and occupation. All I had to do was look in the eyes of a seven-year-old girl who ran to me to ask for my rations, day after day until she was shot dead, to know that the people we intimidated, beat, detained, and killed were human beings with the same hungry stomachs as my American-born children.

When I finally abandoned my country and entered Canada, I had to continue to leave behind a number of attitudes I barely knew I had. My grandfather—the man who had passed on the good values that helped me find my own conscience in Iraq—was not a perfect man. He was an out-and-out racist, as a matter of fact, and he believed that Asian people were the enemies of Americans. When Brandi, the children, and I crossed the border at Niagara Falls, New York, we drove to Toronto and stayed for six months—at no charge—in the home of Winnie and Eugene Ng, two Asian Canadians.

I hadn't known many gentle caregivers in my early years in Oklahoma. In a way, Winnie and Eugene became caring parents to Brandi and me. Our own boys called them "Grandma Winnie" and "Grandpa Eugene." All I had to do was spend one hour at the table of Winnie and Eugene to realize how sadly mistaken was my grandfather in his blind hatred of Asian people. Grandfather Elmer, too, had been to war. He had fought in Korea. I imagine that he had found it necessary to demonize and hate the people he fought. But I don't have to keep my grandfather's demons alive. And I don't have to nourish the prejudices I was taught in my own training in the American army.

Because I fought an unconventional war in Iraq, and because that war brought me into close contact with ordinary civilians who were struggling to survive—in the very ways that Americans would be struggling to survive, if the tables were turned—I was able to slowly awaken to the humanity of the very people I was told to despise. Coming to Toronto and staying with Winnie and Eugene moved me along the same path. It showed me how easy it was to put my grandfather's demons to sleep. That is one less demon for me to pass on to my children.

If every American soldier set aside his or her M-249 automatic rifle and sat down to dinner with an Iraqi family, I believe that the house raids the next day would be a tad less brutal. If the dinners continued, perhaps the house raids would come to an end. I believe that even the most patriotic soldiers in my company would hesitate to beat up, zipcuff, and arrest a sixteen-year-old boy if they discovered that the teenager liked falafels and mint tea and studied trigonometry in the hope that one day, if the universities open up again, he might be able to learn from the brightest minds still alive in his country.

The War Resisters Support Campaign is a Toronto-based group with volunteers around the country. They help out the thirty or so deserters who, like me, have applied for refugee status in Canada. They provided food for my family during our first several months in their country. I did my best to pay them back by speaking at public events about my experiences in Iraq.

I will never forget the first time I was asked to speak in public. It was at a meeting of the Canadian Labour

Congress, just a month or so after we arrived in Toronto. I was so terrified that I could barely open my mouth. Eventually, I grew into public speaking. In the summer of 2005, Brandi, the children, and I drove from Toronto to the Pacific Coast and back, stopping for me to give talks in some twenty towns and cities along the way. I spoke in churches, mosques, libraries, and community halls. I met with journalists everywhere I went. All I wanted to do was tell people what I had seen and done and why I had chosen to desert the American army in Iraq.

I especially liked speaking in mosques. I was worried the first time that I might be received with hatred and accusations. But each time I have visited a mosque, I have been received warmly and encouraged to speak about my experiences at war and why I deserted the army. I can never undo the things I did in Iraq. I will always have to live with them. But I live with them a little easier when I reach out and speak to Muslims in Canada. I tell them that I am sorry about what I did to their brothers and sisters, and that I hope they can find it in their hearts to forgive me. Prospects for peace do not look good in the world, but I believe that individual citizens can make a difference. For my part, I speak to as many people as I can about the things I did and saw in Iraq. I am grateful to break bread with Muslims when they invite me to meet with them.

Although some Canadians have disagreed with me, and one man in British Columbia even threatened to put me in a boat and drag me to the American border, most of the people I've met in this country have treated me well. Yet it remains to be seen whether I will be allowed to stay in Canada. Just as this book was going to press, the Canadian Immigration and Refugee Board rejected my application for refugee status. However, I am appealing that decision in court and will not give up my fight until I have explored every avenue to make Canada a permanent home for my wife, our children, and myself. I also believe that the other men and women who have deserted the American armed forces because they do not wish to serve in Iraq should be allowed to stay in Canada. I believe that it would be wrong for Canada to force me to return to a country that ordered me repeatedly to abuse Iraqi civilians and that was later found to be torturing and humiliating inmates at Abu Ghraib prison. I don't think it's right that I should be sent back to do more of the same in Iraq, or that I should serve jail time in the United States for refusing to fight in an immoral war.

Some thirty years ago, under the leadership of the late Pierre Trudeau, the Canadian government welcomed draft dodgers from the Vietnam War. The current Canadian government, led by Prime Minister Stephen Harper, has not looked favorably on such refugee claims made by recent deserters of the American army. My case is unusual because I am the first deserter in Canada to argue that I went AWOL after being ordered to take part in a steady stream of human rights violations in Iraq. Still, I am not optimistic about my future, and it is challenging to live in shadows of doubt. At some point soon, I could be told to pack my bags and leave. Any day now, my family could be completely torn apart.

If I have any choice in the matter, I will not return to the United States. I have lost my country, and it has lost me. I would reconsider this position only if the United States prosecuted President Bush and all the senior military officials responsible for sending our army into Iraq. I would be willing to sit in a jail cell with the president, for instance, but I would not use my hands on him. Much as I think the man deserves a licking, I'm through with physical abuse—in Oklahoma, in American boot camps, in Iraq, and everywhere else in the world. If I were alone in a jail cell with George W. Bush, I would use words with the man and try to talk some sense into his head.

If given the chance to have a man-to-man talk with the president of the United States, I would tell him to take a look at the laws and the constitution of his own country. He needs to know that during the time I served in the war in Iraq, soldiers and officers of the American forces violated the very values that we claim to uphold in our own nation. If the president wishes to know exactly what values I am talking about, I would direct him to some of the first words of the American Declaration of Independence of 1776: *We hold these truths to be self-evident, that all men are created equal, that they are endowed by their Creator with certain unalienable Rights, that among these are Life, Liberty and the pursuit of Happiness.*

Although I would love to sit down with the president, I would like even more to have half an hour with every young American who is thinking of signing up for the poverty draft. As poor and as desperate as my young family was when I drove to the armed forces recruiting center in Oklahoma in March 2002, I never would have signed up if I'd known I would be blasting into Iraqis' houses, terrorizing women and children, and detaining every man we could find—and all that for $1,200 a month as a private first class. Somehow, somewhere, I would have found a job and a way to survive. I never would have gone to war for my country if I had known what my country was going to do at war in Iraq.

Young people need to know that they don't have to live with the moral anguish of fighting an immoral war. It is not true that a soldier's first obligation is to the military. One's first obligation is to the moral truth buried deep inside our own souls. Every person knows what is right and wrong. And we have a duty to live up to it, regardless of what our leaders sometimes say.

When I came home from Iraq I was a complete wreck. I had so many nightmares that I had to get a prescription for pills to help stave off the bad dreams. I had blackouts. I would cry one moment and scream the next. I was so paranoid that the simple act of standing in line in a grocery store seemed fraught with peril: somebody, surely, would pull out a gun or rip the pin from a grenade. Every day, I thought of the civilians I had seen arrested, beaten, or killed in Iraq. I could not focus. I could not sit still with a child on my lap. I could not deal with the sound of my own children crying, laughing, and calling out for my love. My son Zackary grabbed on to me for dear life in an effort to prevent me from disappearing back into "Sergeant World," but I barely knew how to respond to his love or give it back to him. I was but a shell of the man who had left the United States just seven months earlier, and I intend always to remember that my wife, Brandi, loved me and encouraged me and stuck with me even when it meant that we all had to go into a long period of hiding, insecurity, and poverty. I participated in hurting the people of Iraq, and I paid a price for it. And I wasn't the only one.

When I came home I told Brandi that I had seen innocent people die in Iraq. For the longest time, that is just about all she knew. But because she loved me that was all she needed to hear. In fact, she did not want to hear any details. Taking care of three young boys and me, as well as little Anna, who was soon growing in her womb, Brandi did not feel she had the strength to hear about everything I had seen and done in Iraq. Apart from one time in Philadelphia when I got drunk and began to shout about the young girl I had seen killed outside the hospital in Ramadi, I have never spoken to her directly about all the intimate details given in this book. She read the information form I gave the Canadian immigration authorities when I applied for refugee status. When she put it down, she said she never would have read it in the first place if she had known what she'd find in it. We both carry emotional wounds as a result of the war in Iraq, and I imagine that thousands of other Americans who served in Iraq have also brought their own nightmares back home. Their families, too, will be suffering. Ordinary Iraqis have paid very dearly for this war, and ordinary Americans are paying for it too with their lives and with their souls.

I have never been a man to run from a challenge, and I have never fled from danger or abandoned vulnerable people. I am neither a coward nor a traitor. When I was being recruited in Oklahoma City in 2002, I had to sign a paper to the effect that I had read and understood a warning from the military: "Desertion in the time of war means death by a firing squad." That just about sums it up. We could do whatever we wanted to Iraqis. Yet if we ran from duty, there would be hell to pay. I will never apologize for deserting the American army. I deserted an injustice and leaving was the right thing to do. I owe one apology and one apology only, and that is to the people of Iraq.

At Al-Qa'im one morning after a night of guard duty

On top of an armored personnel carrier with another soldier

At the border with Syria near Al-Qa'im

Author's Note

WE WISH TO ACKNOWLEDGE THE CLOSE COLLABORATION
that led to the writing of this book, and to thank the people
who helped us.

  After hearing Joshua Key speak on CBC radio in
the spring of 2006, the Canadian literary agent Denise
Bukowski contacted him and asked if he would like to
write a book about his experiences as an American soldier
in Iraq. In April 2006, Joshua Key and Lawrence Hill
began to work together. The project began with a series
of in-depth interviews conducted in British Columbia, the
Canadian Prairies, and the Toronto area. Between these
intensive sessions, the two were in touch regularly by telephone and e-mail while Lawrence sifted through hundreds

of pages of notes and dozens of taped interviews and began to write Josh's story. As the book took shape, Joshua reviewed every line many times to ensure that it accurately reflected his experiences, observations, and beliefs. Of the numerous incidents during his service in Iraq, he was extremely careful to recount only what he saw and experienced himself.

Both authors are grateful to their literary agent, Denise Bukowski, for the enthusiasm with which she brought this book to the attention of publishers in numerous countries. We offer special thanks to Morgan Entrekin and Amy Hundley at Atlantic Monthly Press in New York and to Lynn Henry at House of Anansi Press in Toronto, for their commitment and courage in standing behind this book and bringing it to market.

—Joshua Key and Lawrence Hill

I thank my mother, Judy Porter, and brother, Tyler Barker, for believing in me during and especially after my service with the American army in Iraq. I also want to thank Michelle Robidoux and her colleagues at the War Resisters' Support Campaign in Toronto, my lawyer, Jeffry House, and Winnie and Eugene Ng, Neil and Ruth Loomis, Al and Marjorie Stewart, Lynn Wytenbroek, and Elaine for their generous support. Many other people across the United States and Canada showed kindness to my family and me in times of need, and I thank all of them too.

—Joshua Key

It has been an honor to work with Joshua Key and to write his story. I thank Joshua and Brandi for the trust they placed in me during our many conversations. As well, I wish to thank my wife, Miranda Hill, for her unwavering support and encouragement.

—Lawrence Hill